nebraska symposium on motivation
1963

Nebraska Symposium on Motivation, 1963, is Volume XI in the series on CURRENT THEORY AND RESEARCH IN MOTIVATION

nebraska symposium on motivation
1963

MARSHALL R. JONES, Editor

Carl R. Rogers

Professor of Psychology
and Psychiatry
University of Wisconsin

Robert R. Sears

Professor of Psychology and
Dean, School of Humanities
and Science
Stanford University

Neal E. Miller

James Rowland Angell
Professor of Psychology
Yale University

Karl H. Pribram

USPHS Research Professor,
Departments of Psychology
and Psychiatry
Stanford University

H.W.Magoun

Professor of Anatomy
and Dean, Graduate College
*University of California,
Los Angeles*

university of nebraska press
lincoln
1963

Publishers on the Plains

UNP

Copyright © by the University of Nebraska Press
Library of Congress catalog card number 53–11655
Manufactured in the United States of America

Contents

Introduction

It is with considerable difficulty that I address myself to the task of writing the introduction to this, the eleventh volume in the series of Nebraska symposia on motivation. Securing participants for these symposia, seeing the manuscripts of the papers through to their publication, and especially the opportunity to interact intellectually, professionally and socially with the scientists who have presented papers in this series has been a rich and rewarding experience. The group who participated in the symposium this year is no exception. It would be difficult to find a more stimulating and more pleasant group than Carl Rogers, Henry Murray, Robert Sears, Neal Miller, Karl Pribram and Horace Magoun. Furthermore, the response to this series on a national, and even international basis, has been far greater, and therefore more rewarding, than I anticipated when I started the series eleven years ago. It is, therefore, with genuine regret that I find it necessary, because I have accepted a position at another university, to terminate my association with these symposia with this volume.

For several years I have been trying to get Carl Rogers to discuss the motivational aspects of his theory in this symposium. His paper in this volume does this very well. He sees, as anyone familiar with his theory will know, the directional tendency in every living organism of maintaining, enhancing and reproducing itself as fundamental to the question of motivation. This "actualizing" tendency is *the* motivational construct in his theory. It involves development toward autonomy and away from heteronomy, or control by external forces. In earlier formulations, Rogers has recognized that the tendency to actualize the organism is, in man, often in conflict with tendencies to actualize the self. Originally he related this to an incongruence between the self-perceptions held by the individual and his organismic experiencing. In this paper, Rogers develops the alternative view that this rift between experience and self-perception is something learned through cultural conditioning in which behaviors which are perversions of the natural directions of the unitary actualizing tendency are rewarded and reinforced. He also develops some fascinating ideas about the implications of this view for self-awareness, seeing the latter as an indication of trouble which has as its function the elimination of the trouble and the reduction of self-awareness.

Sears reports some of the results of his more recent research on the problems of dependency and relates these results to the earlier findings obtained in his Iowa and Harvard studies. The paper he presents in this volume is a logical extension of his earlier work and an integral part of his continued program of research in the importance of parent-child relationships in the development of personality. He reports here evidence that indicates that there are significant differences in the dependency behaviors of boys and girls, and that different antecedent conditions underlie these behaviors. He also reports that the various measures of dependency which he has used in his studies do not correlate well with each other and he concludes that dependency probably is not a unitary concept.

Miller presents one of the best summaries that I know about of the various types of reinforcement theories, indicates succinctly the strengths and weaknesses of each, outlines the as yet unresolved problems in this field, and then offers a new theory of his own. He starts by questioning his original assumption that increased vigor of a response related to pain reduction, after the pain stops, in the effect of reinforcement due to drive reduction. He explores instead, the implications which follow from making the assumption that sudden relief from pain produces an automatic increase in the activity of any neural circuits that have just been firing and that this energization is responsible for the strong performance which in turn is responsible for learning by contiguity. The assumption of the possibility of the existence of such a "go mechanism" leads to a large number of very exciting ideas and the delineation of a host of reasearchable problems. This is a very significant contribution by one of the best scientists in this field which is, in itself, one of the central areas in modern psychology.

Pirbram's paper is another highly significant contribution to the analysis of the reinforcement problem. He early makes the point that reinforcements are event sequences that occur in the context of other event sequences. He then points out that there is ample evidence for a process in the nervous system against which incoming signals are matched. This process is built up through previous experience and it "may be conceived as a coded representation of prior signals generated by organism-environment interaction; ... it is subject to alteration by signals of mismatch; ... it leads to 'expectancies' of the environment by the organism." Conceptualized this way, contiguity of stimuli is seen as a process occurring as a context-content relationship and, in the nervous system at least, essentially similar to expectancy theory. But there also is evidence, behaviorally and neurophysiologically, that the context-content relationship can be reversed as a function of experience. This makes it possible to explain some of the problems involved in drive-stimulus and drive-reduction hypotheses. As Pribram says, "On this basis, the suggestion is made that the outcomes of actions initially biased *by* drive stimuli can, through experience, come *to* bias them." He also examines the implications of this model for performance theory, particularly in the areas of addictance and effectance, and for perceptual performance. All of this is well buttressed with references to research, his own and that of others, from a wide variety of sources and much of which may not be familiar to most psychologists. Finally, Pribram examines the relation of these kinds of events and processes to the subjective feelings which accompany them. He says, "The suggestion is made that happiness is slowly achieved through the progressive gain in control over stimulus events, through the structuring of con-sequent performances, that is, through reinforcement. In the course of human existence, many moments recur when control reaches the point, just before the reorganization of satiety, when sensitivity is maximal. At such moments, 'happiness is a warm puppy'."

Magoun has addressed himself to a fundamental problem in motivation that none of the other 66 participants in this series has dealt with in anything more than a passing way. That is the problem of how behavior, once it is started, gets stopped. He

summarizes a tremendous amount of research literature on inhi-
bition, relating the research evidence to central neural inhibition,
to external inhibition, habituation, internal inhibition, thalamo-
cortical mechanisms for internal inhibition, the bulbar driving
of the thalamo-cortical system, satiety and internal inhibition,
and sleep. Although this is an area in which my own knowledge
of the literature is limited, I suspect it is safe to say that Magoun's
paper includes the most thorough and readable summary of the
literature on central neural inhibition and contains the most
provocative insights and suggestions for future research in this
area that is generally available in the psychological literature.
Many of the papers presented in these symposia have turned
out to be landmarks of considerable significance in the develop-
ment of theory and research in various areas of psychology.
Magoun's paper will, I am sure, be another.

Another participant in the symposium this year was Henry
Murray, certainly one of the most eminent of our senior psycholo-
gists by any standards. He made a highly significant contribution
to the symposium in the speech he gave, in his participation in
the discussion which followed his presentation and those of Carl
Rogers and Robert Sears, in his most stimulating discussions
with individual students and staff members, and in his gracious
participation in the various social activities that have come to
be associated with these symposia. I know therefore that those of
you who were able to attend the symposium in person, as well as
those of you who follow it through these annual volumes, will
share with me the disappointment attendant upon the fact
that it was not possible for Professor Murray to prepare a formal
paper. His contribution to the symposium was considerable and
we all regret the combination of circumstances which makes it
impossible for him to have a paper in this volume.

In behalf of the Department of Psychology, I should like to
take this opportunity to express appreciation to the National
Institute for Mental Health for the grant which has made these
symposia possible. I should also like to express gratitude to Vice
Chancellor Adam C. Breckenridge who, by cutting through
some of the usual institutional red tape and by making available
a small amount of funds this year, enhanced the teaching func-

tions of the symposia considerably by making it possible for us to hold them in surroundings much more suitable than would otherwise have been available. The staff of the University of Nebraska Press, and especially Mr. Bruce Nicoll, Director, deserve kudos also for the cooperation which has made it possible to make these symposia available to a much wider audience than could possibly attend the meetings each year.

For myself, I should like to take this opportunity to express my appreciation not only to those mentioned above, but also to the 66 scientists who have participated in these symposia in the last 11 years, to the many psychologists who have helped me keep aware of the significant work being done by the many scientists working in the area of motivation, to the graduate students who have told me of the intellectual stimulation they have received from the symposia, and to the great many psychologists in America and Europe who have expressed their interest in and satisfaction with the series.

Those of you who have followed this series will be as happy as I am to know that the Department of Psychology has elected to continue these symposia and they will be organized under the leadership of my good friend and able colleague, Professor David Levine.

MARSHALL R. JONES

Lincoln, Nebraska
June 15, 1963

The Actualizing Tendency in Relation to "Motives" and to Consciousness

CARL R. ROGERS

University of Wisconsin

THE ACTUALIZING TENDENCY

THIS PAPER, in its later sections, contains many ideas and beliefs which are at this point tentative and uncertain in me. They may therefore be the most profitable for discussion and clarification. This first section, however, presents a conviction which has grown stronger in me over the years. I should like to introduce it by telling of an experience, very remote from psychology, which made a strong impression on me.

During a vacation weekend some months ago I was standing on a headland overlooking one of the rugged coves which dot the coastline of northern California. Several large rock outcroppings were at the mouth of the cove, and these received the full force of the great Pacific combers which, beating upon them, broke into mountains of spray before surging into the cliff-lined shore. As I watched the waves breaking over these large rocks in the distance, I noticed with surprise what appeared to be tiny palm trees on the rocks, no more than two or three feet high, taking the pounding of the breakers. Through my binoculars I saw that these were some type of seaweed, with a slender "trunk" topped off with a head of leaves. As one examined a specimen in the

NOTE: The author is indebted to many persons in the writing of this paper, but would like to acknowledge special indebtedness to Lancelot L. Whyte, for valuable conversations at the Center for Advanced Study in the Behavioral Sciences, and to Wesley Westman for stimulating suggestions.

1

intervals between the waves it seemed clear that this fragile, erect, top-heavy plant would be utterly crushed and broken by the next breaker. When the wave crunched down upon it, the trunk bent almost flat, the leaves were whipped into a straight line by the torrent of the water, yet the moment the wave had passed, here was the plant again, erect, tough, resilient. It seemed incredible that it was able to take this incessant pounding hour after hour, day and night, week after week, perhaps, for all I know, year after year, and all the time nourishing itself, extending its domain, reproducing itself; in short, maintaining and enhancing itself in this process which, in our shorthand, we call growth. Here in this palmlike seaweed was the tenacity of life, the forward thrust of life, the ability to push into an incredibly hostile environment and not only to hold its own, but to adapt, develop, become itself.

Now I am very well aware that we can, as we say, "explain" many aspects of this phenomenon. Thus we can explain that the weed grows on top of the rock rather than on the protected side, because it is phototropic. We can even attempt some biochemical explanations of phototropism. We can say that the plant grows where it does because there is an ecological niche which it fills, and that if *this* plant had not developed to fill this niche, the process of evolution would have favored some other organism which would gradually have developed much these same characteristics. I am aware that we can now begin to explain why this plant assumes the form it does, and why if it is damaged in some storm, it will repair itself in a way consistent with its own basic species-form. This will all come about because the DNA molecule, as long as it is a part of, and is interacting with, a living cell, carries within it, like a program for guiding a computer, instructions to each emergent cell as to the form and function it will assume in order to make the whole a functioning organism.

Such knowledge *explains* nothing, in any fundamental sense. Yet it is very valuable as a part of the continuing differentiation, the finer description, the more accurate picture of functional relationships, which our curiosity demands, and which gives us at least a deeper respect for and understanding of the complexities of life.

But my reason for telling this story is to call attention to a more general characteristic. Whether we are speaking of this sea plant or an oak tree, of an earthworm or a great night-flying moth, of an ape or a man, we will do well, I believe, to recognize that life is an active process, not a passive one. Whether the stimulus arises from within or without, whether the environment is favorable or unfavorable, the behaviors of an organism can be counted on to be in the direction of maintaining, enhancing, and reproducing itself. This is the very nature of the process we call life. Speaking of the totality of these reactions within an organism Bertalanffy says: "We find that all parts and processes are so ordered that they guarantee the maintenance, construction, restitution, and reproduction of organic systems" (Bertalanffy, 1960, p. 13). When we speak in any basic way of what "motivates" the behavior of organisms, it is this directional tendency, it seems to me, which is fundamental. This tendency is operative at all times, in all organisms. Indeed, it is only the presence or absence of this total directional process which enables us to tell whether a given organism is alive or dead.

It was considerations of this kind which led me to formulate the actualizing tendency as the motivational construct in my own theory of personality and therapy (Rogers, 1959). I was influenced in my thinking by the work of Goldstein, Maslow, Angyal, and others. I wrote of the actualizing tendency as involving "development toward the differentiation of organs and functions, expansion and enhancement through reproduction. It is development toward autonomy and away from heteronomy, or control by external forces" (Rogers, 1959, p. 196).

Although it was ten years ago that I worked out this formulation (there was a long lag before publication), I have found no reason to change this basic notion of the process underlying all behaviors. Indeed, there seems to have been an increasing degree of support for a conception of the organism as an active directional initiator. The "empty organism" school of thought, with nothing intervening between stimulus and response, is on the decline.

Only after attempting to formulate my own theory did I become aware of some of the work in biology which supported the concept of the actualizing tendency. One example, replicated with different species, is the work of Driesch with sea urchins many years ago, quoted by Bertalanffy (Bertalanffy, 1960, p. 5). He learned how to tease apart the two cells which are formed after the first division of the fertilized egg. Had they been left to develop normally it is clear that each of these two cells would have grown into a portion of a sea urchin larva, the contributions of both being needed to form a whole creature. So it seems equally obvious that when the two cells are skillfully separated, each, if it grows, will simply develop into some portion of a sea urchin. But this is overlooking the directional and actualizing tendency characteristic of all organic growth. It is found that each cell, if it can be kept alive, now develops into a whole sea urchin larva—a bit smaller than usual, but normal and complete.

I am sure that I choose this example because it seems so closely analogous to my experience of dealing with individuals in psychotherapy. Here, too, the most impressive fact about the individual human being seems to be his directional tendency toward wholeness, toward actualization of his potentialities. I have not found psychotherapy effective when I have tried to create in another individual something which is not there, but I have found that if I can provide the conditions which make for growth, then this positive directional tendency brings about constructive results. The scientist with the divided sea urchin egg is in the same situation. He cannot cause the cell to develop in one way or another, he cannot (at least as yet) shape or control the DNA molecule, but if he focuses his skill on providing the conditions which permit the cell to survive and grow, then the tendency for growth and the direction of growth will be evident, and will come from within the organism. I cannot think of a better analogy for psychotherapy where, if I can supply a psychological amniotic fluid, forward movement of a constructive sort will occur.

Support for the concept of an actualizing tendency comes at times from surprising quarters, as in the simple but unusual experiments of Dember, Earl, and Paradise, which show that rats prefer an environment involving more complex stimuli over an environment involving less complex stimuli. It seems striking that even the lowly laboratory rat, within the range of complexity that he can appreciate, prefers a more richly stimulating setting to a more impoverished one. The authors' theory states, and is thus far confirmed, that "a shift in preference, if it occurs, will be unidirectional, toward stimuli of greater complexity" (Dember, Earl, and Paradise, 1957, p. 517).

Better known are the increasing number of studies having to do with exploratory behavior, curiosity, play—the spontaneous tendency of the organism to seek stimulation, to produce a difference in the stimulus field (Berlyne, 1960; Harlow, 1953, are examples). This concept has become well accepted during the past decade.

The work in the field of sensory deprivation underscores even more strongly the fact that tension reduction or the absence of stimulation is a far cry from being the desired state of the organism. Freud (1953, p. 63) could not have been more wrong in his postulate that "the nervous system is . . . an apparatus which would even, if this were feasible, maintain itself in an altogether unstimulated condition." On the contrary, when deprived of external stimuli, the human organism produces a flood of internal stimuli sometimes of the most bizarre sort. As Goldstein (1947, p. 141) points out, "The tendency to discharge any tension whatsoever is a characteristic expression of a defective organism, of disease."

Much of the material summarized by White (1959) in his excellent article on motivation adds up to the point I too have been making, namely, that the organism is an active initiator and exhibits a directional tendency. He puts this in very appealing terms when he says, "Even when its primary needs are satisfied and its homeostatic chores are done, an organism is alive, active, and up to something." (White, 1959, p. 315)

As a consequence of these and other developments in psychological and biological research, I feel considerably more secure than I did a decade ago in calling attention to the significance of those directions in the human organism which account for its maintenance and enhancement.

I would like to add one comment which may be clarifying. Sometimes this tendency is spoken of as if it involved the development of all of the potentialities of the organism. This is clearly not true. The organism does not, as Leeper has pointed out, tend toward developing its capacity for nausea, nor does it actualize its potentiality for self-destruction, nor its ability to bear pain. Only under unusual or perverse circumstances do these potentialities become actualized. It is clear that the actualizing tendency is selective and directional, a constructive tendency if you will.

Thus, to me it is meaningful to say that the substratum of all motivation is the organismic tendency toward fulfillment. This tendency may express itself in the widest range of behaviors, and in response to a very wide variety of needs. Maslow's hierarchy of needs manages to catch something of the fact that certain wants of a basic sort must be at least partially met before other needs become urgent. Consequently, the tendency of the organism to actualize itself may at one moment lead to the seeking of food or sexual satisfaction, and yet unless these needs are overpoweringly great, even these satisfactions will be sought in ways which enhance rather than diminish self-esteem. And other fulfillments will also be sought in the transactions with the environment—the need for exploration, for producing change in the environment, for play, for self-exploration when that is perceived as an avenue to actualization—all of these and many other behaviors are basically "motivated" by the actualizing tendency.

We are, in short, dealing with an organism which is always motivated, is always "up to something," always seeking. So I would reaffirm, perhaps even more strongly after the passage of a decade, my belief that there is one central source of energy in the human organism; that it is a function of the whole organism rather than of some portion of it; and that it is perhaps best conceptualized as a tendency toward fulfillment, toward actualization, toward the maintenance and enhancement of the organism.

WHO NEEDS "MOTIVES"?

At this point, however, I should like to introduce an idea which, if it has gained some limited acceptance during recent years, is still far from being acceptable to most psychologists. I can introduce it by posing this question. Given the motivational substratum of the actualizing tendency, is anything added to our theories by postulating more specific motivational constructs? How helpful has it been in the past and how helpful is it likely to be in the future to specify and try to give meaning to a variety of special motives? I am not arguing that these differing types of seeking do not take place. Men do seek food, and they do tend toward increasing their competence in dealing with the environment, and most people wish to increase their self-esteem, but I am not at all sure that there is any profit to thinking of a hunger motive, a competence motive, or a self-esteem motive. Are these heuristic concepts? Do they lead to significant discovery? Are they provocative of effective research? Obviously I am dubious.

As I endeavor to discover what constitutes science in its truest sense, it seems to me clear that science has not made progress by positing forces, attractions, repulsions, causes, and the like, to explain *why* things happen. As we all know, there are very few answers to the question "why." But science has progressed and found itself on more fruitful paths when it restricts itself to the question of "how" things happen. When the theory was offered that nature abhors a vacuum, and that this explained *why* air rushes in to fill any vacuum or partial vacuum, this led to little effective research. But when science began to describe, in empirical terms, the functional relationships which hold between a partial vacuum and the atmospheric pressure outside the container, significant results accrued, and the question as to whether nature feels this particular abhorrence was forgotten. Or, as Galileo so forcefully demonstrated, when we cease trying to formulate the reasons as to *why* a stone falls, and concentrate on the exact description of its rate of fall per second, and the degree of its acceleration, then these exact descriptions of functional relationships open up whole new fields of investigation and are incredibly fruitful of further knowledge. One of the by-products is a loss of interest in *why* the stone falls.

In the same vein, I doubt if psychologists make progress in their science so long as their basic theory focuses on the formulation that man seeks food *because* he has a hunger motive or drive; that he interacts in an exploratory and manipulative manner with his environment *because* he has a competence motive; that he seeks achievement *because* he has a mastery drive or a need for achievement. Even in the area that has seemed so clear to so many, the concept of a sexual motive has not been too helpful in unraveling the vastly complex variables which determine sexual behavior even in animals—the genetic, physiological, environmental, maturational, social, perceptual, and other elements which enter in. As Beach (1955, p. 409) has pointed out in regard to instincts, such concepts of specific energy sources lead to oversimplified theories and even to an insistence upon theories rather than upon observation. His proposal regarding the improvement of the situation regarding instincts bears consideration in regard to motives:

> The analysis that is needed involves two types of approach. One rests upon determination of the relationships existing between genes and behavior. The other consists of studying the development of various behavior patterns in the individual, and determining the number and kinds of factors that normally control the final form of the response.
>
> When these methods have been applied to the various types of behavior which today are called "instinctive," the concept of instinct will disappear, to be replaced by scientifically valid and useful explanations.

In much the same fashion I believe that when we have developed and tested hypotheses as to the conditions which are necessary and sufficient antecedents to certain behaviors, when we understand the complex variables which underlie various expressions of the actualizing tendency of the organism, then the concept of specific motives will disappear.

An Illustration

The point I am making could be illustrated from many areas of psychology but you will not be surprised if I speak of it from the area of my own work. I would like to sketch briefly a chain of experiences in theory and research regarding the therapeutic relationship, and endeavor to relate these experiences to what I have been saying about motivational constructs.

In a lifetime of professional effort I have been fascinated by the process of change which sometimes occurs in human beings in the therapeutic relationship when it is, as we say, "successful." Individual clients in such a relationship could be described in very general and theoretical terms as moving in the direction of actualization of their potentialities, moving away from rigidity and toward flexibility, moving toward more process living, moving toward autonomy, and the like. In more specific and empirical terms we know that they change in their observed behaviors, exhibiting more socially mature behavior, that they change in the way in which they perceive themselves, that they place a more positive value upon self, that they give more healthy responses to projective tests. Perhaps it should be stressed that these generalizations regarding the direction of the process in which they are engaged exist in a context of enormously diverse specific behaviors, with different meanings for different individuals. Thus, progress toward maturity for one means developing sufficient autonomy to divorce himself from an unsuitable marriage partner; in another it means living more constructively with the partner he has. For one student it means working hard to obtain better grades; for another it means a lessened compulsiveness and a willingness to accept poorer grades. So we must recognize that the generalizations about this process of change are abstractions drawn from a very complex diversified picture.

But the nagging question over the years has been What is it that initiates this process? Every therapist knows that it does not occur in each of his clients. What are the conditions, in the client, in the therapist, in the interaction, which are antecedent to this process of change? In trying to formulate hypotheses in regard to this, I believe that there is no substitute for close observation—with as much openness to unexpected facts and possibilities as the observer can bring to bear, with as much laying aside of defensiveness and rigidity as he can achieve. As I continued to observe therapy, the formulation at which I gradually arrived was very different from the views with which I started, though how much defensive inability to see the facts is still involved no man can say of himself. At any rate, the theoretical position to which I came hypothesized that the process of change was initiated primarily by the psychological climate created by the therapist, and not by his techniques, his therapeutic orientation, or his scholarly knowledge of personality dynamics. I have spelled out these hypotheses in different publications (Rogers, 1962a, 1959, 1957).

The point to which I would call attention is that when you become interested in the conditions which are antecedent to a given complex of behaviors, it becomes quite clear that questions regarding specific motives seem futile as leads for further work. Are differing therapist behaviors due to varying degrees of altruistic motive? or to differing amounts of the need for affiliation? or to the need for dominance? Are the client's behaviors due to his competence motive? or his need for dependence? or is there a self-exploration motive which is tapped? To me these do not seem to be heuristic questions.

On the other hand, when I begin, on the basis of observation, to hypothesize specific conditions or determinants of change, then, it seems to me, research progress is stimulated in two ways. In the first place, one attempts to describe the specific conditions which appear to operate, not to consult a list of motives. The specific conditions may conceivably be genetic or physiological or environmental. They may be strictly observable behaviors, or may be phenomenological states inferred from the behaviors. They may be interactional, although in my experience interactional variables are difficult to make operational. In the second place, it is, I believe, considerably easier to give operational definitions of observed conditions than to measure a general motivational state such as need for affiliation.

In any event, to continue with my account, the conditions which appeared on the basis of observation to be antecedent to and relevant to the process of developmental change in the client, were of quite different sorts. There were essentially five—four of them attitudinal sets in the therapist, one an element in the client.

An accurate and sensitive empathy communicated by the therapist appeared crucial. This is a variable which falls in the class of directly observable behaviors. It has been possible to assess it from the verbal behavior of the therapist and from his vocal inflections.

The warmth of positive regard for the client experienced by the therapist was postulated as a second variable of significance.

This is a complex factor existing in the phenomenal field of the therapist, which may be inferred from the quality and tone of his voice. It can also be inferred from his posture and gestures, if moving pictures or direct observation can be employed.

Third, the unconditionality of the therapist's regard is a related factor deemed to be important. Is the therapist's regard relatively conditional, that is, valuing certain aspects of the client and his behavior, and devaluing other aspects, or is it unconditional? Assessment of such a variable must to some degree be an inference regarding the phenomenal field of the therapist, but to the extent that the regard is conditional, it constitutes observable behavior, evident in verbalizations, inflections, gestures.

A fourth element hypothesized to be important was the congruence of the therapist—the extent to which, in the relationship, he is integrated, whole, real, his conscious attitudes and behavior congruent with the experiencing going on in him. Assessment must be based entirely on behavioral observation—the voice qualities particularly—since a lack of congruence is usually unknown to the therapist himself at the time, being essentially a defense against feelings in himself which he senses as threatening. Thus, this seems like an extremely subtle assessment to make. We are assisted in this, however, by the fact that this type of assessment is made by every one from childhood up, as he evaluates each relationship as to whether the person is being real, or is acting a role, putting up a façade, or being a "phony."

The fifth and final condition is purely phenomenological—the client's perception of at least a minimal degree of these qualities in the therapist. We have used a paper-and-pencil inventory to get at this client perception.

Now it should be clear that these are very crude formulations of variables hypothesized to be significant. In this respect they are, I believe, representative of the primitive state of psychological science as it relates to human beings. It is a tragedy that we have not achieved any rational scientific methodology which is adequate for the study of organisms with their wholistic nature and their basic process characteristics. So these formulations I have given represent only a first awkward attempt to define the elements which nourish and facilitate psychological change, growth, development toward maturity, in the human person. I see them as roughly analogous to the early attempts to isolate the nutritional elements which promote physical growth. Just as a maturing science can now define with very considerable precision the elements necessary for physical growth, so I believe a maturing psychological science will eventually define the psychological nutriments which promote personal growth.

When I ask myself if this attempt would have proceeded more rapidly or more accurately if we had hypotheses based upon some theory of specific motives, rather than upon naturalistic observation, my answer is strongly negative. In my judgment, assessment of therapist motives, such as need for affiliation, for altruism, for dominance or mastery or competence, would have approached only very indirectly, if at all, the problem of the conditions which facilitate change. And if I turn the question around and ask myself what motive lies behind the therapist's genuineness or his sensitive empathy in the relationship, I must answer that I do not know. Nor does the question have any real importance for me. So I reiterate the idea voiced previously, that a theory involving specific motivations, no matter how they are categorized or sliced, does not seem to me to be helpful in the empirical investigations which alone can determine the patterning which exists in human behavior.

Yet when the variables are selected through subjective observation, when the scientist is willing to use his own disciplined sensitivity to his experience in the selection of variables, when he is willing to trust his experience as a tentative and perhaps intuitive guide in the formulation of hypotheses, positive results can emerge. I think we often fail to recognize the truth of Polanyi's (1958) thesis that if it were not for the pattern which the disciplined scientist senses long before he can confirm or disconfirm it, there would be no such thing as an advancing science.

So to complete very briefly the story of these particular formulations about the conditions necessary for the therapeutic process, I will attempt to summarize the results of a number of completed studies in this field, several of which are moving toward publication (Barrett-Lennard, in press; Halkides, 1958; Spotts, 1962; Truax, 1962, Truax, Liccione and Rosenberg 1962). The studies deal with two rather different groups of clients: on the one hand, students and other adults who come voluntarily for help; and on the other hand, schizophrenic individuals who have been in a state hospital for periods ranging from a few months to many years. The first group is above the socio-educational average, well motivated, and ranging from mildly to seriously disturbed in their functioning. The second group is below the socio-educational average, not only unmotivated but resistant, unable to cope with life in the community, and often out of contact with reality.

In the different studies there have been three ways of measuring the relationship elements I have described. The first method is through the rating of brief segments of the recorded interviews, usually four minutes in length, taken in a randomized fashion from the interview. Raters, listening to these segments, judge the degree to which the therapist is, for example, being accurately empathic, and make a rating on a carefully defined scale. The raters have no knowledge as to whether the segment is from an early or late interview, or a more or less successful case. In the most recent of the studies a different group of raters has made the ratings for each of the qualities.

A second method of measurement has been through the use of the Relationship Inventory, an instrument designed to capture the client's perception of the qualities of the relationship. The third method is also based on this Inventory, filled out by the therapist to obtain *his* perception of the relationship qualities.

Various criteria of change have been used in these studies, to assess the degree of positive or negative change in personality. In all cases the criteria of change have been independent of the measures of the attitudinal elements. Some of the measures have been: assessment by clinicians, working "blind," of the changes between pre- and post-projective and other tests; changes in various MMPI scales; changes in Q-sort adjustment score and in a measure of anxiety. There have also been measures of process movement in some of the studies, based upon a process analysis of the interview segments made entirely independently of the attitudinal assessment.

The major finding from all of the studies is that clients in relationships marked by a high level of therapist congruence, empathy, and positive regard of an unconditional sort, tend to show a significant degree of constructive personality change and development. Clients in relationships characterized by a low level of these attitudinal conditions show significantly less positive change on the indices described above. In the schizophrenic group, the individuals in relationships low in these qualities show *negative* personality change. They are, at the end, worse off than their matched nontherapy controls. Clinically, this is a very sobering finding; scientifically, it is of great importance. There are various other findings which are of interest but not relevant to our present topic.

I have given this much of the findings simply to indicate that variables abstracted from observation, quite without regard to motivational constructs, have proven to be significantly related to personality change. They are of the order which I believe has usually been of the most importance in science, namely "x is a function of y." In this case, personality change is a function of certain measured relationship qualities.

But this is not all. One of our staff has also abstracted out the construct of client likability, and has shown that the likability of the client is also associated with the degree of change (Stoler, in press). Again, motivational constructs have, I am sure, played no part in this research. In some further work we seem to be teasing out a factor which perhaps we could call client readiness, as still another predictor of change. What I am saying is that in our efforts to understand objectively a complex process of change in the personality and behavior of the individual we are making progress, but that progress has in no way come from theories of specific motivations. In fact, to have operated from a base of such theories would, I believe, only have clouded the difficult task of discovering the elements which, empirically, are associated with change.

A Restatement

Let me summarize very briefly what I have been saying up to this point. The human organism is active, actualizing, and directional. This is the basis for all of my thinking. Once this fact is accepted, I see no virtue in imposing abstractions regarding specific motives upon man's complex and multiform behavior. It is certainly possible to categorize the behavioral phenomena into many different motives and, in fact, these phenomena may be sliced in a variety of ways, but that this is desirable or heuristic seems dubious to me. I have tried to indicate by illustration that in any actual attempt to understand the conditions antecedent to behavior it may be preferable to formulate our hypotheses on the basis of close observation of the phenomena, rather than upon a previously constructed series of motives.

The Problem of Incongruence or Dissociation

I should like now to turn to a very different and very puzzling cluster of questions. These questions are certainly related to the issue of motivation, but to many other aspects of personality theory as well. Anyone who delves at all into the dynamics of human behavior must deal with them in some way. I have myself found them very perplexing, and have felt quite dissatisfied with the all too easy "explanations" which have been given. They have to do with what I think of as incongruence or dissociation. In general, the questions are of this sort. How is it that man is so frequently at war within himself? How do we account for the all too common rift which we observe between the conscious aspects of man and his organismic aspects? How do we account for what appears to be two conflicting motivational systems in man?

To take a very simple example, how is it that a woman can consciously be a very submissive and compliant person, very sure that this is her goal, that such behavior represents her true values, and then at times blow up in abnormally hostile and resentful behavior which greatly surprises her, and which she does not own as a part of herself? Clearly her organism has been experiencing both submission and aggression, and moving toward the expression of both. Yet at the conscious level she has no awareness and no acceptance of one aspect of this process going on within her. This is a simple example of the rift with which every psychologist interested in human behavior must come to terms.

In the theory I advanced a decade ago I saw the rift as an incongruence between the self-perceptions held by the individual and his organismic experiencing. I said that this was brought about by distorted perceptions of self and experience, which in turn grew out of conditions of worth introjected from significant others. I expressed the view that the actualizing tendency promoted the fulfillment of the organism on the one hand, but that as the self developed it also tended to actualize the self, and that frequently the self and the experience of the organism were decidedly incongruent. Thus, we have the actualizing tendency splitting into two systems at least partially antagonistic in their directions (Rogers, 1959, pp. 196–97). I am not at all sure that this captures the facts in the way most effective for promoting investigation. I do not see any clear solution to the problem, but I think perhaps I see the issues in a larger context. So I should like to share my puzzlement with you. To do so, I would like to back away and look at the broad picture.

In nature, the working out of the actualizing tendency shows a surprising efficiency. The organism makes errors, to be sure, but these are corrected on the basis of feedback. Even the human infant, faced with natural, unflavored foods, does a quite satisfactory job of balancing his diet over time, and thus both maintains and enhances his development. This type of relatively integrated, self-regulating behavior, directed toward maintenance and fulfillment, seems to be the rule in nature rather than the exception. One can, of course, point to serious mistakes over evolutionary time. Evidently the dinosaurs, by becoming very efficiently and rigidly actualized in terms of a given environment, could not adapt, and thus effectively destroyed themselves through the perfection with which they had fulfilled themselves in a given environment. But this is the exception. On the whole, organisms behave in ways which make an awesome degree of directional sense.

In man, however—perhaps particularly in our culture—the potentiality for awareness of his functioning can go so persistently awry as to make him truly estranged from his organismic experiencing. He can become self-defeating as in neurosis, incapable of coping with life as in psychosis, unhappy and divided as in the maladjustments which occur in all of us. Why this division? How is it that a man can be consciously struggling toward one goal, while his whole organic direction is at cross purposes with this?

In puzzling over this issue, I find myself trying to take a fresh look at the place and function of awareness in the life of man. The ability to focus conscious attention seems to be one of the latest evolutionary developments in our species. It is, we might say, a tiny peak of awareness, of symbolizing capacity, based on a vast pyramid of nonconscious organismic functioning. Perhaps a better analogy more indicative of the continual change going on, is to think of man's functioning as a large, pyramidal fountain in which the very tip of the fountain is intermittently illuminated with the flickering light of consciousness, but the constant flow goes on in darkness or in the light.

In the person who is functioning well, awareness tends to be reflexive, rather than the sharp spotlight of focused attention. Perhaps it is more accurate to say that in such a person awareness is simply a reflection of something of the flow of the organism at that moment. It is only when the functioning is disrupted that a sharply self-conscious awareness arises. Speaking of the different aspects of awareness in this well-functioning person, I have said, "I do not mean that this individual would be self-consciously aware of all that was going on within himself, like the centipede who became aware of all his legs. On the contrary, he would be free to live a feeling subjectively, as well as be aware of it. He might experience love or pain or fear, living in this attitude subjectively. Or he might abstract himself from this subjectivity and realize in awareness, 'I am in pain'; 'I am afraid'; 'I do love.' The crucial point is that there would be no barriers, no inhibitions, which would prevent the full experiencing of whatever was organismically present" (Rogers, 1962b, p. 25).

In this way, as in various other ways, my thinking is similar to that of Lancelot Whyte, who comes at the same problem from a very different perspective, that of the philosopher of science and historian of ideas. He too feels that in the person who is functioning well "the free play of spontaneous vitality—as in the transitory rhythms of eating, drinking, walking, loving, making things, working well, thinking, and dreaming—evokes no persistent differentiated awareness. We feel right while it is going on, and then forget it, as a rule" (Whyte, 1960, p. 35).

When functioning in this manner the person is whole, integrated, unitary. This appears to be the desirable and efficient human way. Sharpened self-consciousness in such functioning arises, according to Whyte, only as a result of contrast or clash between the organism and its environment, and the function of such self-awareness is to eliminate the clash by modifying the environment or altering the behavior of the individual. His viewpoint is startling but challenging when he says, "The main purpose of conscious thought, its neobiological function, may be first to identify, and then to eliminate, the factors which evoke it" (Whyte, 1960, p. 37).

It will probably be evident that such views as the foregoing could be held only by individuals who see the nonconscious aspect of man's living in a positive light. I have myself stressed the idea that man is wiser than his intellect, and that well-functioning persons "accept the realization that the meanings implicit in their experiencing of a situation constitute the wisest and most satisfying indication of appropriate behavior." They have come to "trust their experiencing" (Rogers, 1962b, p. 28). Whyte places this same idea in a larger context when he says, "Crystals, plants, and animals grow without any conscious fuss, and the strangeness of our own history disappears once we assume that the same kind of natural ordering process that guides their growth also guided the development of man and of his mind, and does so still" (1960, p. 5). It is clear that these views are very remote from Freud's distrust of the unconscious, and his general view that it was antisocial in its direction. Instead, as developed in these paragraphs, when man is functioning in an integrated, unified, effective manner, he has confidence in the directions which he unconsciously chooses, and trusts his experiencing, of which, even if he is fortunate, he has only partial glimpses in his awareness.

If this is a reasonable description of the functioning of consciousness when all is going well, why does the rift develop in so many of us, to the point that organismically we are moving in one direction, and in our conscious life are struggling in another?

I am interested that Whyte and I give sharply different explanations of the way in which this dissociation comes about, but very similar descriptions of the condition itself. A brief summary can scarcely do justice to his thought, but he believes that the tendency of European or Western man to lose his proper organic integration has come about through the peculiarly Western development of static concepts—in the formation of our language, in our thought, in our philosophy. Though nature is clearly process, man has been caught in his own fixed forms of thought: "Deliberate behavior was organized by the use of static concepts, while spontaneous behavior continued to express a formative process; that special part of nature which we call thought thus became alien in form to the rest of nature . . ." (Whyte, 1949, p. 39). It is in this fashion, he believes, that a dissociation develops in which "mutually incompatible systems of behavior compete for control" (Whyte, 1949, p. 44). It is his judgment that this rift is more profound in men than in women because for various reasons, woman's special functions "link her thought more closely to those organic processes which maintain the animal harmony" (Whyte, 1949, p. 40).

My own explanation has more to do with the personal dynamics of the individual. Love by the parent or significant other is made conditional. It is given only on the condition that the child introject certain constructs and values as his own, otherwise he will not be perceived as worthwhile, as worthy of love. These constructs are rigid and static since they are not a part of the child's normal process of evaluating his experience. He tends to disregard his own experiencing process wherever it conflicts with these constructs, and thus to this degree cuts himself off from his organic functioning, becoming to this degree dissociated. If the conditions of worth imposed on him are numerous and significant, then the dissociation can become very great, and the psychological consequences serious indeed (Rogers, 1959, pp. 221–33).

I have gradually come to see this dissociation, rift, estrangement, as something learned, a perverse channeling of some of the actualizing tendency into behaviors which do not actualize. In this respect it would be similar to the situation in which sexual urges can, through learning, be channeled perversely into behaviors far removed from the physiological and evolutionary ends of these impulses. In this respect my thinking has changed during the past decade. Ten years ago I was endeavoring to explain the rift between self and experience, between conscious goals and organismic directions, as something natural and necessary, albeit unfortunate. Now I believe that individuals are culturally conditioned, rewarded, reinforced, for behaviors which are in fact preversions of the natural directions of the unitary actualizing tendency. As Whyte says, "The conflict between spontaneous and deliberate behavior would never have represented more than a normal difficulty of choice had the influence of the social tradition been favorable to the maintenance of the overriding coordination" (1949, p. 44).

Both Whyte and I see the end result as similar, in that dissociated man is best described as man consciously behaving in terms of static constructs and abstractions and unconsciously behaving in terms of the actualizing tendency. This is in sharp contrast to the healthy, well-functioning person who lives in close and confident relationship to his own ongoing organismic process, nonconscious as well as conscious. I see constructive outcomes in therapy and Whyte sees constructive developments in society as possible only in terms of the human individual who trusts his own inner directions and whose awareness is a part of and integrated with the process nature of his organic functioning. Whyte states the goal as being "the recovery of animal harmony in the differentiated form appropriate to man at this stage of history" (1949, p. 199). I have described the functioning of the psychologically mature individual as being similar in many ways to that of the infant, except that the fluid process of experiencing has more scope and sweep, and that the mature individual, like the child, "trusts and uses the wisdom of his organism, with the difference that he is able to do so knowingly" (Rogers, 1962c, p. 14).

Let me endeavor to summarize my thoughts on this matter. I have said that the extremely common estrangement of conscious man from his directional organismic processes is not a necessary part of man's nature. It is instead something learned, and to an especially high degree in our Western culture. It is characterized by behaviors which are guided by rigid concepts and constructs, interrupted at times by behaviors guided by the organismic processes. The satisfaction or fulfillment of the actualizing tendency has become bifurcated into incompatible behavioral systems, of which one may be dominant at one moment, and the other dominant at another moment, but at a continual cost of strain and inefficiency. This dissociation which exists in most of us is the pattern and the basis of all psychological pathology in man, and the basis of all his social pathology as well. This, at least, is my view.

The natural and efficient mode of living as a human being, however, a mode partially achieved by individuals whom we term psychologically mature, does not involve this dissociation, this bifurcation. Instead, such a person exhibits a trust in the directions of his inner organismic processes which, with consciousness participating in a coordinated rather than a competitive fashion, carry him forward in a total, unified, integrated, adaptive, and changing encounter with life and its challenges.

I trust that the significance which I attach to the function of the actualizing tendency is indicated by the preceding paragraph. The tragic condition of man is that he has lost confidence in his own nonconscious inner directions. Again, I cannot refrain from quoting Whyte's words which express my own view: "Western man stands out as a highly developed but bizarre distortion of the human animal" (1949, p. 46). To me the remedy for this situation is the incredibly difficult but not impossible task of permitting the human individual to grow and develop in a continuing confident relationship to the formative actualizing tendency and process in himself. If awareness and conscious thought are seen as a part of life—not its master nor its opponent, but an illumination of the developing processes within the individual—then man's total life can be the unified and unifying experience which seems characteristic in nature. If man's magnificent symbolizing capacity can develop as a part of and guided by the tendency toward fulfillment which exists in him as in every creature, then the "animal harmony" is never lost, and becomes a human harmony and human wholeness simply because our species is capable of greater richness of experience than any other.

And if the skeptical and natural question is raised, "Yes, but how? How could this possibly come about?" then it seems to me that the illustration I gave of research regarding the therapeutic relationship is a very small but hopefully a significant signpost in this respect. Our capacity for scientific investigation can help us. It seems very probable that the conditions which promote dissociation, which bifurcate the actualizing tendency, can be empirically identified. I have pointed out two types of hypotheses already formulated by Whyte and myself, which lie at hand for testing. The conditions which are associated with the restoration of unity and integration in the individual are, as I have indicated, already in process of being identified. The conditions which would promote a continuing internal harmony in children, without the all too common learning of dissociation, can also be identified and put to preventive use. We can, if we will, I believe, use our scientific skills to help us keep man whole and unified, a creature whose actualizing tendency will be continually forming him in the direction of a richer and more fulfilling relationship to life.

SUMMARY

I have endeavored to say three things. First, there is a tendency toward fulfillment which is the most basic aspect of the life of any organism. It is the substratum of anything we might term motivation.

Second, I have questioned whether the formulation of theories of specific motives moves us forward in research. Since the major usefulness of theories is to stimulate research, I question the value of specific motivational constructs. Through an illustration, I have endeavored to indicate that the determinants of any given set of complex behaviors may perhaps be more accurately hypothesized from careful naturalistic observation than from thinking in terms of "motives."

Third, and finally, I have pointed out that in nature the actualizing tendency usually brings about a unified and integrated behavioral process, often highly complex in character. Why in man does it so often produce bifurcated systems—conscious versus unconscious, self versus the experiencing process, conceived values versus experienced values? I have hypothesized that this is due to specific types of social learning, especially predominant in Western culture, and not a *necessary* part of human living. If this type of learning is not a necessary element of human life, there would seem to be some possibility that it might be changed.

REFERENCES

Barrett-Lennard, G. T. Dimensions of therapist response as causal factors in therapeutic change. *Psychol. Monogr.* in press.

Beach, F. A. The descent of instinct. *Psychol. Rev.*, 1955, **62**, 401–410.

Berlyne, D. E. *Conflict, arousal, and curiosity.* New York: McGraw-Hill, 1960.

Bertalanffy, L. *Problems of Life.* New York: Harper Torchbooks, 1960 (first published 1952).

Dember, W. N., Earl, R. W., & Paradise, N. Response by rats to differential stimulus complexity. *J. comp. physiol. Psychol.*, 1957, **50**, 514–518.

Freud, S. Instincts and their vicissitudes. *Collected Papers.* London: Hogarth Press and Inst. of Psychoanalysis. Vol. IV, 1953. Pp. 60–83.

Goldstein, K. *Human nature in the light of psychopathology.* Cambridge: Harvard Univ. Press, 1947.

Halkides, G. An experimental study of four conditions necessary for therapeutic change. Unpublished doctoral dissertation, Univ. of Chicago, 1958.

Harlow, H. F. Motivation as a factor in the acquisition of new responses. *Current Theory and Research in Motivation: A symposium.* Lincoln, Neb.: Univ. of Nebraska Press, 1953. Pp. 24–49.

Polanyi, M. *Personal knowledge.* Chicago: Univ. of Chicago Press, 1958.

Rogers, C. R. The interpersonal relationship: the core of guidance. *Harv. Educ. Rev.*, 1962a, **32**, 416–429.

Rogers, C. R. The necessary and sufficient conditions of therapeutic personality change. *J. consult. Psychol.*, 1957, **21**, 95–103.

Rogers, C. R. A theory of therapy, personality, and interpersonal relationships. In S. Koch (Ed.). *Psychology: A Study of a Science.* New York: McGraw-Hill. Vol. III, 1959. Pp. 184–256.

Rogers, C. R. Toward becoming a fully functioning person. In *Perceiving, behaving, becoming,* 1962 Yearbook, Assoc. for Supervision and Curriculum Dev. Washington, D. C.: Nat. Educ. Assn., 1962b, 21–33.

Rogers, C. R. Toward a modern approach to values. Unpublished manuscript, 1962c.

Spotts, J. E. The perception of positive regard by relatively successful and relatively unsuccessful clients. Wisconsin Psychiatric Institute: Research Reports, 1962. Unpublished manuscript.

Stoler, N. Client likability: a variable in the study of psychotherapy. *J. consult. Psychol.,* in press.

Truax, C. B. The relationship between the level of accurate empathy offered in psychotherapy and case outcome. Wisconsin Psychiatric Institute: Research Reports, 1962. Unpublished manuscript.

Truax, C. B., Liccione, J., & Rosenberg, M. Psychological test evaluations of personality change in high conditions therapy, low conditions therapy, and control patients. Wisconsin Psychiatric Institute: Research Reports, 1962. Unpublished manuscript.

White, R. W. Motivation reconsidered: the concept of competence. *Psychol. Rev.,* 1959, **66**, 297–333.

Whyte, L. L. *The next development in man.* New York: Mentor Books, 1949.

Whyte, L. L. *The unconscious before Freud.* London: Tavistock Publications, 1960.

Dependency Motivation

ROBERT R. SEARS

Stanford University

DEPENDENCY is one of the most significant, enduring, and pervasive qualities of human behavior. From birth to old age, it influences the form and quality of all dyadic relationships. Yet, for some curious reason—perhaps because Freud failed to discriminate it from object cathexis—this behavior system has never had the microscopic analysis by intensive, theory-oriented clinical study that has so well informed us on the genetics and dynamics of sex and aggression. For an understanding of dependency, therefore, we must turn to other kinds of theory and investigation. My intention is to present here some comments on certain theoretical issues that are relevant to this motivational system, and then to report some recent empirical findings about its genetics as these are revealed by correlations between child-rearing experiences and the intensity of children's dependency behavior in their fifth year of life.

DEPENDENCY AS MOTIVATION

I have referred to dependency as a motivational system. This is simply a convention, and may be more confusing than explicative. There is a less-than-charming ambiguity about the term *motivation*. Originally, it meant the *sources of motion*, but several camels have crept under the tent in recent years. This extension of meaning—or at least of usage—was inevitable for the very reasons that led to the term's popularity in the first place. To make these reasons clear, I must go back a couple of centuries.

British associationism offered an almost purely sensory and cognitive account of mental processes. The "springs of action" were ignored. When the nineteenth century brought a broadened conception of the subject matter of psychology, with *conduct* replacing *mental process,* the problem of motive had to be faced. The times were out of joint for the British philosophers, however, and the notion of conation had no sooner been introduced for the purpose of handling the internal initiation of action than the whole matter was made moot by the victory of scientific psychology over the armchair variety.

The particular segment of the new science that was relevant to conduct developed from the work of the German objective physiologists and culminated in American behaviorism. Its style was analytic; its outcome was the molecularization of the reference events it sought to study. Conation was translated into motivation, and research was directed toward the physiology of drives.

Drives were not enough, however. By the mid-twenties, it had become apparent that the physiological reductionism of Watson, Cannon, and others of their generation left out of account the complex, socially oriented and peculiarly human kinds of striving that had formed the useful core of such armchair systems as that of McDougall. Hunger and thirst were amenable to precise research, but that was their chief virtue. They were poor models for comprehending love, hate, aspiration, competition, dependency, and gregariousness.

It was at this point that Freud's conceptualization of the libido came to the rescue. Following the biological Zeitgeist of the late nineteenth century, he had conceived of a sexual motive having qualities of recurrence and action-induction similar to the qualities of the hunger and thirst motives, but with an important difference—libido was an instinct, not just a drive, and hence Freud gave more attention to the associated action, the strivings toward goals, the objects of attachment, the developmental sequence of zones and object choices, and the transformations of these things under various circumstances, than he did to the drive quality itself. Indeed, the latter was scarcely more than an analogy, and after sixty years still remains so.

There were two consequences of the intrusion of the libido model in psychological theory. The first was that attention now became focused on a total action system instead of just its internal instigator. Virtually every current formulation of behavior organization and dynamics concerns itself with (1) the nature of instigation to some substantively defined group of actions, (2) the conditions under which these actions develop, (3) the nature of the goals they reach, and (4) the organization of the actions into structures. The main reference event for the student of molar behavior is no longer a hypothetical motive, but a whole action system. This addition of actions, object choices, goals, and traits is what I meant by saying that in recent years some camels had got into the tent of motivation. *Drive* has been joined by several other constructs relating to the substantive rubric by which a particular drive is labelled.

The second consequence of the libido model was less fortunate. The reason the libido seemed helpful was that it preserved the fiction of drive. The theoretical similarity to the physiologically defined drives was evident and comforting. It made for an easy transition to the action system approach because it retained the familiar biological substrate of motive. By the mid-thirties, some kind of drive concept was firmly embedded in most thinking about action systems, as witness the *needs* of Murray (1938) and the *secondary drives* of the Hullian descendants (e.g., Dollard *et al.*, 1939), and remained largely unquestioned until quite recently. Perhaps this is not surprising, for the hardest things to remove from any theory—or even to question effectively—are pure constructs which are unsusceptible to direct investigation or measurement. This is not to say that drive *should* be removed from behavior theory, but only that it has persisted too long without proper examination.

The behavior system of dependency provides a case in point. It represents one of the action systems that have replaced the many motives of neobehaviorism or the instincts of an even earlier day. A contemporary examination of any substantively defined behavior system requires attention to the principles which concern three of its aspects: genetics, dynamics, and structure. Naturally, one wants a theoretical framework within which the various empirical discoveries about dependent behavior will fit amicably. A proper question to ask is: what does the term *dependency* define, or refer to, within the range of systematic constructs we use currently for describing molar behavior systems? Is it a drive, or a set of precisely (or imprecisely) defined actions, or a trait, or what?

This question has been in the air for several years and has led to vigorous argument as to whether *drive* is a necessary construct at all and, if so, how it can be defined. Some investigators have conceptualized dependency as a secondary drive, an intervening variable modeled quite directly after such primary drives as hunger and sex. Presumably, this view has been taken because of the spontaneous character, and persistence, of young children's seeking for attention, affection, and reassurance from their parents, the seeming increase in strength of such supplication when nurturance or affection is withheld, and the reduction of such striving when a substantial amount of nurturance has been given. If we acknowledge, as we must, that there is no critical evidence to support the drive conception, then we must ask what alternative explanations can be used to account for these phenomena. Recently, Gewirtz (1961) has presented a persuasive argument for the view that dependent behavior is, rather, an operant activity in response only to those cues that have previously been associated with the reinforcements that followed dependent supplication (and presumably to cues, also, that function for stimulus generalization). He finds no need for a drive construct, but rests with a statement of stimuli and learned responses. The differential implications of these two interpretations have yet to be derived in the kind of detail that will permit an empirical determination of where the truth lies.

One fact must be kept in mind. Whichever theory ultimately proves most efficient, the data from which inferences are made come always from *observations of overt dependent behavior.* For the moment, we will keep the drive theory as one of two reasonable possibilities, recognizing clearly that the overt behavior from which such a hypothetical construct is inferred is nevertheless learned according to the same principles as those that govern the strengthening and weakening of operant actions in response to cue stimuli. Whether *drive* instigation is an economical addition to the list of external and internal cues that elicit dependent behavior, will have to be decided on the basis of some other data than those we have presently available.

DEFINITION OF DEPENDENCY

In its current usage, the notion of dependency as a motive stems mainly from two sources, Murray's *n* succorance (1938) and Whiting's analysis of help-seeking as a reaction to frustration (1944). Murray described succorance as being behaviorally exemplified by crying or pleading for nourishment, love, aid, and protection; the need was not limited to food, but included the associated caretaking and affectional nurturance that go with both infant feeding and other forms of infant care.

Whiting also emphasized the oral quality of dependency, suggesting that the association of hunger gratification with supportive and help-giving maternal behavior led to the development of an acquired drive for which such behaviors were the appropriate rewards. Whiting pointed to the inevitability of dependency supplication as a reaction to frustration; since the satisfaction of early food needs was associated with affectionate care, later frustrations served as cues to elicit the same kind of supplication for help that had been learned initially. Thus, while Murray made point of the drive (or need) quality of dependency, Whiting added another step and specified an external state of affairs (frustration) that could activate dependency behavior.

The conditions under which dependent behavior is presumed to be established in a child have been described in detail by Sears, Maccoby, and Levin (1957). They mainly involve the child's interaction with his original caretaker. The mother's caretaking behavior provides both the manipulanda required for the child's responses and the reinforcing stimulation that shapes those responses into a stable pattern of dependent behavior. On the child's side, there are operant responses from the beginning; the first of these are limited largely to sucking or mouthing movements, clutching and grasping reflexes, seemingly random vocalizations, and postural adjustments to being moved and held.

On the mother's side, the operant behavior is very complex, of course, since it is designed to achieve many caretaking ends—feeding, bathing, cleansing, warming, and so on—and many mother-gratifying experiences such as cuddling, fondling, being clutched at and sucked at, hearing, smelling, even tasting the baby.

On neither side do we have a truly definitive list of these actions, even for one mother-baby pair, nor have we much notion as to the similarities and differences across individuals or cultures. At the moment, we can do no better than use examples, such as those above, to redintegrate for each reader his own casual observations of the interaction topography. This is a terrain of almost infinite variety, so far as the mother is concerned, but since her behavior is constantly guided by the conscious and unconscious purposes of her actions, this operant multiplicity channels into controlling-systems that have definite shaping value for the baby's behavior. His operant repertoire increases as his capacities for more complex and directed behavior mature, and as the reinforcements of certain movements multiply, and those of others disappear.

One apparent result of this mutually satisfying relationship is the creation of secondary rewards or reinforcers for both members of the pair. That is, the mother's talking, patting, smiling, her gestures of affection or concern, are constantly being presented to the baby in context with primary reinforcing stimulations such as those involved in eating, fondling, and caressing.

A second consequence of mother-baby interaction is the development of expectancies on the part of both members. Each learns to respond to the other's smiles, posture, and other acts, not only with reactions suitable to the manipulandum and stimulus properties of the behavior, but also with an expectation of subsequent events.

The child's expectancy is an inferred internal response to signals from the mother, and is essential to the chaining of his responses into purposeful units of activity. If the mother fails to perform the expected act from her own repertoire, the baby will suffer frustration and express resentment by crying or thrashing about or whatever he has so far learned to do in frustrating circumstances. Thus, to use oral frustration in the nursing situation as an example, if the mother performs all the initial acts that normally culminate in placing the nipple in the child's mouth, but then hesitates at the critical instant—interrupting the flow of her own behavior and hence not performing the environmental event that is reciprocal to the child's flow of behavior—an angry bellow is likely to ensue. The development of mutual expectancies molds the mother and baby into a dyad, a unit which can operate effectively only so long as both members perform their accustomed roles in expected fashion.

For the child, the upshot of this infantile experience is that a certain number of operant responses become firmly established to the various instigators that have been commonly associated with primary gratifications or reinforcing stimuli. The child learns to "ask" for the mother's reciprocal behavior. *These asking movements are the dependency acts whose frequency and intensity we use as a measure of the dependency trait (or action system).* More precisely, we assume that the effectiveness of this learning process varies under different conditions and schedules of reinforcement, and that therefore children differ in the amount and kinds of such behavior.

If this view is correct, then there should be certain predictable relationships between parental child rearing practices and children's dependency behavior. First, the greater the reinforcement of dependency behavior in infancy, the greater should be the frequency at age four to five. Second, the greater the current reinforcement (or, at least, permissiveness) at this latter age, the greater should be the frequency. And finally, the greater the frustration of dependency behavior, the more frequently it should occur in the neutral and nonpunitive setting represented by the nursery school. These simply stated hypotheses require further explanation, but first let me describe briefly a naturalistic study from which data may be drawn to test them; then further discussion of the hypotheses can be incorporated with the presentation of findings.

A Study of Dependency

In connection with a rather elaborate, and as yet unpublished, study of the child-rearing correlates of identification, data were obtained on four-year-old children's dependency behavior in a nursery school setting.[1] During an eight-week summer session of

[1] This study was performed at Stanford during the summer of 1958. The senior staff in charge of the project were Lucy Rau, Richard Alpert, and

the Stanford Nursery School, 40 children (21 boys and 19 girls) were observed in free play for 7 to 10 hours each. Their behavior was recorded in terms of five categories of dependency, which is our main concern here, and several categories of both aggression and adult role behavior. The observations were made by a time-sampling procedure with half-minute units; these were taken in groups of 20, that is, 10 minutes of observation of a given child at one time. The scheduling of these observation periods provided careful randomizing of such variables as time of day, time during the week, and which of the four observers was assigned. Observer reliability, measured during the first, fourth and seventh weeks, was quite satisfactory.

The final measures of dependency, which are to be used for studying child rearing correlates, are *frequency* measures. For each of the children, we have a score on each of the five dependency categories; this score is the proportion of the total number of the child's half-minute observation periods during which a given category of dependency was displayed. The five categories of dependency were as follows:

Negative Attention Seeking: Getting attention by disruption, aggressive activity with minimal provocation, defiance, or oppositional behavior (e.g., opposes and resists direction, rules, routines, and demands by ignoring, refusing, or doing the opposite).

Positive Attention Seeking: Seeking praise, seeking to join an in-group by inviting cooperative activity, actual interruption of an ongoing group activity.

Touching or Holding: Nonaggressive touching, holding, clasping onto others.

Being Near: Follows or stands near a particular child or a group of children or a teacher.

Robert Sears. A monograph report is in preparation. The present description of the procedures relating to dependency is designed only to give the reader an understanding of the types of data secured, and makes no pretence of completeness. The final report will contain a full description of sampling, observer reliability, child consistency, nature of scoring, category definitions, and methods of observing.

Seeking Reassurance, Comfort, or Consolation: Apologizing, asking unnecessary permission or for protection or for help or guidance.

Total Observed Dependency: The sum of all five categories, each weighted in accord with its raw frequency.

Information about the child-rearing experiences of the children was obtained by interviewing their mothers and fathers. The mother inteviews were similar to those reported in *Patterns of Child Rearing,* but had somewhat greater emphasis on moral training and on relationships of the child with the father. The father interviews were much the same as the mother interviews, but excluded discussion of infant feeding and toilet training. The interviews were recorded, transcribed, and coded in the same ways as the *Patterns* interviews.

Finally, a few measures of dependency were obtained in two half-hour sessions of a somewhat structured mother-child interaction. The mother was instructed as to the simple tasks or occupations to be performed during the periods, and the pair were then left alone while observers recorded both mother and child behavior from behind a one-way mirror.

The data to be reported here are mainly correlations of two kinds—those among the several measures of child dependency, and those between the child measures and parental ratings obtained from the parent interviews or mother-child interactions.

SEX DIFFERENCES

So far as sheer frequency is concerned, there is only one category that shows a significant sex difference. In Table 1 are shown the mean frequency scores, by sex, on all the dependency measures, together with standard deviations of the distributions, and the *p* value (based on *t*) for those differences that were of moderate size. Only *negative attention seeking* shows a difference. These findings are similar to those reported in an earlier study done at Iowa (Sears *et al.,* 1953), except that the difference favoring boys on negative attention seeking, in that study, was negligible. Perhaps this was a result of the fact that the girls in that research

TABLE 1

Dependency Measures: Means, Standard Deviations, and Sex Differences

Measure	Var. No.	Boys		Girls		Diff.: Boys-Girls	p
		Mean	S.D.	Mean	S.D.		
Negative attention	187	3.19	2.34	1.79	1.36	1.40	.025
Reassurance	188	3.86	2.12	4.89	2.38	−1.03	.17
Positive attention	219	5.19	2.42	5.05	2.52	.14	n.s.
Touching & holding	220	3.90	2.78	3.74	2.53	.16	n.s.
Being near	221	3.67	2.53	4.58	2.89	−.91	n.s.
Total dependency	224	5.14	2.44	5.89	3.16	−.75	n.s.
Mother-child dependency	335	5.67	2.36	5.21	2.17	.46	n.s.
Bid for attention: mother busy	336	5.14	1.67	4.21	1.88	.93	.11
Bid for attention: mother attentive	337	2.67	1.32	2.63	1.53	.04	n.s.

group, as was noted on the basis of doll play aggression measures, were somewhat more aggressive than the usual Iowa nursery school population. Since negative attention seeking is significantly correlated with amount of interpersonal aggression expressed, a variation in sampling could have masked the difference which was revealed more clearly in the present group.

Organization of Dependency

The fact that the nonaggressive forms of dependency were not different in *frequency* for the sexes must not be allowed to minimize the importance of sex role in relation to dependency, however. In Table 2 are shown the intercorrelations among the several measures, separately by sex of child.

In general, those among the five observation categories center around zero for the boys but are mainly small and positive for the girls. The slightly higher interrelationships for the girls are represented also by the higher correlations of the separate categories with their sum, called *total dependency;* the median for the boys is .45, for the girls, .61.

TABLE 2

Dependency: Intercorrelations Among Measures (Girls Above the Diagonal, Boys Below)

Measures		187	188	219	220	221	224	335	336	337
Negative attention	187		06	10	15	37	29	-13	-15	37
Reassurance	188	-24		25	19	26	56	-10	-09	44
Positive attention	219	23	-11		11	-03	62	10	23	62
Touching & holding	220	04	14	-16		71	61	-14	19	44
Being near	221	-03	12	-14	13		67	-04	23	42
Total dependency	224	20	39	46	45	56		06	31	71
M-c: dependency	335	02	-28	-07	27	-07	-02		74	10
M-c: bids for attention Q	336	09	06	28	-04	-21	12	33		12
M-c: bids for attention P	337	05	15	-32	-04	22	04	18	00	

The positive relations between the two categories *touching and holding* and *being near,* and the slight negative relation of these with *positive attention* in boys, is reminiscent of the finding by Heathers (1955) that the former two categories are relatively immature forms and *positive attention* is a more mature form. Within the narrow age range of the present group, there is little evidence to support the "mature-immature" dichotomy, and perhaps "active-passive" or "verbal-physical" would be better labels for the contrast. Heathers' characterization of "mature-immature" is doubtless correct, but its significance comes from variations in behavior over longer age ranges than are represented in the present sample.

In general, we must conclude that the five observation categories represent almost entirely independent action systems for boys and show only a very moderate clustering in girls.

The remaining three measures were those obtained during the mother-child interaction. One of these was an over-all dependency rating. For neither sex did this have any significant relation to any other measure of dependency. The other two measures were ratings that combined frequency and intensity into single measures of bids for attention (1) when the mother was busy filling in a questionnaire during the first half of the session, and (2) during a puzzle-solving period in the second session, when the mother was oriented toward the child and was trying to get him to perform skillfully. Among the boys, neither of these showed a significant relationship to any other measure. Among the girls, however, the puzzle-period was significantly correlated with three of the five observation measures. Again, in other words, the girls showed a consistency of dependency expressions and the boys did not.

These findings suggest that the use of such a term as Allport's *common trait* is not warranted in describing the structure or organization of dependent behavior. Rather, each of the five categories needs to be considered separately with respect to its origins.

REINFORCEMENT IN INFANCY

In the search for child-rearing correlates of the children's dependency behavior, we had the three hypotheses mentioned earlier to use as initial guides; one of these related to infancy experiences, and the other two to more prolonged and current conditions. These hypotheses were suggested by the Iowa study, which examined the relation of several child-rearing variables to measures of dependency obtained by both observation and teacher ratings in the nursery school. The present study permits a test of these hypotheses.

One would expect that the more frequently an infant received reward for making dependent responses toward his parents, the more of these responses he would make at age four. This is a deceptively simple hypothesis, however. In fact, the kinds of dependent supplications made during the first year of life drop out almost entirely in the fifth year, and only in the most general sense can "dependency" be compared at the two ages. Hence, the measured responses must be considered to be either products of response generalization or representations of a dependency drive, the strength of which would vary positively with reinforcement. Furthermore, it is an awkward question as to which, if any, of our interview measures of child rearing are reflective of amount of reinforcement.

There are two ways in which reinforcement might vary in infancy. One is through differences in amount of reward given and the other through differences in amount of operant behavior required for a given amount of reward. As an example of the first point, a child separated frequently or continuously from a parent during infancy should have less opportunity to establish dependent responses toward that parent. As an example of the second, scheduled feeding should require more operant activity, with ultimate reward, and hence should create more dependency.

Consider the *amount of reinforcement* first. In Table 3 are given the correlations between the various measures of depend-

TABLE 3

Infancy Experiences: Correlations with Dependency Measures

Dependency Measure	(13) Duration Breast Feeding	(14) Use of Scheduling	(16) Severity of Weaning	(5) (6) Early Separation		(11) (12) Caretaking		Caretaking Part.*	
				Mo.	Fa.	Mo.	Fa.	Mo.	Fa.
GIRLS									
Negative attention	−07	−07	02	15	−23	−49	47	−43	41
Reassurance	−03	−10	04	−06	08	−02	16	02	16
Positive attention	−07	−27	02	−04	−17	−62	17	−61	03
Touching and holding	28	11	−46	07	01	26	22	34	30
Being near	21	−07	−50	−02	−03	13	08	16	12
Total dependency	03	−19	−24	−01	07	−23	16	−20	10
Dependency: m-c	−35	22	12	−04	31	21	−46	12	−43
Bid: mother busy	−28	12	−33	−29	27	12	−31	05	−29
Bid: mother attentive	14	−15	00	02	−21	−29	12	−27	05
BOYS									
Negative attention	43	−19	45	18	−26	11	02	17	14
Reassurance	−31	16	29	−05	08	−37	14	−38	−18
Positive attention	23	08	26	−16	26	18	−49	−26	−51
Touching and holding	−32	−16	−07	28	−23	−41	21	−37	−12
Being near	−21	−22	15	02	03	20	−19	10	−07
Total dependency	−13	−12	38	08	06	−03	−28	−34	−42
Dependency: m-c	08	08	−27	22	29	−06	32	24	39
Bid: mother busy	30	41	−15	−08	18	−34	42	−08	27
Bid: mother attentive	21	00	10	−06	−01	17	23	48	50

*Partial correlations in which the proportional caretaking of the other parent is held constant.

ency and several relevant child-rearing variables. It can be seen that severity of early separation from either parent is unrelated to any significant extent with any of the dependency measures; none of the coefficients reaches the .10 level of significance, and their patterning seems quite random. It should be added that the correlations with each parent's scale are so low, in general, that partial correlations holding each parent scale constant while determining the effects of the other parent alone make no significant changes in the sizes of any of these relationships. Perhaps it would be too much to hope for a relationship here, for there was a quite narrow range of experiences in this respect, as there was in the Iowa study, which provided no indication of a relation between separation and dependency.

A second measure of amount of reinforcement is *duration of breast feeding*. It might be supposed that the longer a child was fed at the breast, the more reinforcement he would receive for his dyadic controlling behavior. The supporting evidence in Table 3 is limited to boys' *negative attention seeking*, which will be discussed later. For the other categories, the relationships are mainly zero or even negative.

Now to turn to the other way of evaluating reinforcement— the proportion of times that a given operant behavior receives reward. The presumption would be that intermittent reinforcement would lead to a stronger response in children, because they would have to perform a greater number of acts to secure reward. In this respect there are two other aspects of infant feeding, besides *duration of breast feeding*, that may be relevant, *scheduling* and *severity of weaning*.

Both were measured and their relations to dependency examined in the Iowa study. There, the extent to which mothers used a self-demand rather than a rigid schedule was interpreted as a measure of the amount of reward the child had received for making supplications. Self-demand, that is, was interpreted as a positive measure of the pure *amount* of reinforcement. However, just the opposite from the expected results were found— the observed dependency in nursery school was somewhat *inversely* related to self-demand feeding, the relation in girls being stronger than in boys. In the present study, this would correspond to a *positive* correlation between *use of scheduled feeding* and *total dependency*. However, reference to Table 3 shows that there was virtually no relation at all between scheduling and any of our observational measures of dependency; the column of coefficients for both sexes strikes us as entirely random in size and direction. The essential point of these results, we believe, is that the findings from the previous investigation are not replicated in the present one.

A second possibly relevant measure of oral experience was *severity of weaning*. The reasoning is that a gentle well-prepared-for weaning to the cup would take into account the child's wishes and provide more frequent reinforcement of supplication with less effort on the child's part than a severe weaning that involved a determined refusal by the mother to respond to the child's requests. Thus, severe weaning would produce dependency. In the Iowa study, observed dependency showed no relation at all to severity of weaning, although rated dependency (by the teachers) was quite clearly *positive* in its relation to weaning severity, as we would expect from the hypothesis. The findings from the present study are equivocal (Table 3); for girls, there was a fairly consistent negative relationship while, for boys, as the hypothesis proposes, the relations were predominantly positive. So far as the Iowa *ratings* of dependency are concerned, then, the Stanford boys replicated the findings, but the girls did not, and indeed were more strongly related in the opposite direction.

Skepticism has been expressed by a number of investigators as to whether there are any detectable influences, in the later nursery school years, of infant oral or feeding experiences. The present findings do nothing to allay such doubts so far as nursery school behavior is concerned. Not only are the expected relationships notably missing, but the relatively small relationships found in the earlier study receive no replication in the present one.

The case is quite different for another (but nonoral) indicator of infant reinforcement, however. The *proportional amount of caretaking* by each parent does provide some rather substantial correlations. These two scales were intended to estimate what proportion of total caretaking was performed by each parent;

sitters and relatives, as well as the other parent, were taken into consideration. They are the same scales used for this purpose in *Patterns*. In the present instance the correlation between the two parents' proportions was −.70 for boys and −.24 for girls; the difference is significant at the .05 level. These correspond to correlations of −.64 and −.46, respectively, in the earlier study, which are not significantly different. These substantial, and differing, correlations between the two parental scales makes partial correlations of some importance in examining these data; the last two columns of Table 3 show partial correlations between the dependency measures and each parent's proportional amount of caretaking with the other parent's proportional amount held constant.

The most notable relation for both sexes is between the observation measure of *positive attention seeking* and the amount of caretaking by the *same-sexed parent;* these correlations are significantly negative, indicating that the greater the proportional amount of caretaking, the less the positive attention seeking in nursery school. Several of the other correlations are rather substantially negative, also, although those for boys' dependency in the mother-child interaction are positive with father caretaking. The over-all indications appear to be in opposition to the hypothesis that amount of caretaking positively reinforces dependency behavior. On the contrary, this parental variable seems to act like a measure of interference or frustration—the less the frustration (higher caretaking), the less the dependency—and the more important influence apparently stems from the same-sexed parent. This finding will be considered further in connection with the discussion of *positive attention seeking* in the next section.

Our conclusion is that the general hypothesis of reinforcement in infancy may or may not be valid, but the present measurements of both child rearing and child behavior variables are unable to demonstrate it. The one antecedent that did show a significant and consistent relationship for both sexes (proportional amount of caretaking by same-sexed parent) was related *oppositely* to the expected direction, and behaved more like a measure of interference than of reinforcement. It seems unlikely that early reinforcement is entirely irrelevant to the development of the cathectic dyadic relation between mother and child, but our measures of dependency are not suitable for estimating cathexis. They are quantitative estimates of operant activity. Such behavior is learned in the context of securing rewarding responses from others, or avoiding punishing ones; its strength (frequency, duration, intensity, resistance to interference) is therefore a function of both the total amount of reinforcement received through the child's entire life history and the amount of internal and external instigation impinging on him at a given time. Furthermore, it is to be expected that the particular dependent acts learned will be the ones permitted or encouraged by the parents, not just a generalized "dependency," and that the concurrent level of excitation and inhibtion of these specific acts will influence their operant strength.

CURRENT REINFORCEMENT AND FRUSTRATION

We turn now to the second and third hypotheses. One says that the greater the current reinforcement by parents, the greater should be the frequency of dependent acts, and the other seems to say just the opposite—that the greater the frustration, the greater the frequency. The inconsistency is only apparent, of course. Reinforcement, as measured by parent scales indicating permissiveness, should increase the habit strength of the dependency acts as responses to parents or to any other person (teachers, children) who are stimulus objects falling on some dimension, with the parents, which provides for stimulus generalization.

Frustration of dependency interactions, as indicated by parental punishment, coldness, or distance, should force the child to work harder—to supplicate more—in order to obtain dyadic rewards. Aperiodic intermittent reinforcement thus operates to increase habit strength. While one might expect the frequency of dependency acts toward the nonresponsive parent to be reduced eventually, we would expect the frequency of such acts in the nonpunitive and accepting nursery school environment to reflect the increased habit strength.

The procedure chosen for analyzing the present data has two purposes. One is to test these two hypotheses; the other is to

discover, if possible, additional antecedents that have not hith-
erto been used in formulating concrete hypotheses. In what fol-
lows, I will present lists of all the correlation coefficients between
each of the five dependency observation measures and the 197
parental measures secured from the interviews and mother-child
interactions that reach a significance level of .05. We can examine
these lists to see whether some of the relationships seem to sup-
port the hypotheses, and what theoretical sense can be made of
those which do not.

This method has some dangers, for it risks capitalizing on
purely chance correlations; there should be about 10 significant
correlations with each dependency measure if there were purely
random correlations among the 197 antecedent measures. Since
these relations are *not* random, there is no way to estimate what
a purely chance yield of .05 level correlations would be. This
seems unimportant, anyway, because we are seeking definite
evidence of permissiveness and frustration, not just random ante-
cedents. In general, the risks of such a procedure can be mini-
mized if one's interpretations of the antecedent variables are
not allowed to stray too far from some preformulated theory.
While this technique of data analysis may be expected to lead
to a quasi-test of the hypotheses, it also serves the second purpose,
which is to increase the precision of the theory by providing new
hypotheses as well as testing old. In this respect, the procedure
is essentially inductive rather than deductive in intent.

NEGATIVE ATTENTION SEEKING

This behavior has an aggressive quality to it, but in the observa-
tion scoring, a disruptive, disobedient, irritating act was cate-
gorized as negative attention rather than aggression if the
observer judged that it was performed mainly to secure atten-
tion. In the Iowa study, there were significant positive correla-
tions for both sexes between *negative attention* and both *total
observed aggression* and the *total of other forms of dependency;*
the relation to aggression in boys was reduced from .49 to .21
when activity level was partialled out, while the same process
for the girls reduced the figure only slightly, from .31 to .27.

In the present study, the relation of negative attention to

TABLE 4

Negative Attention: Correlations with Parent Interview and Mother-Child Interaction Measures at Level $p < .05$

GIRLS

7. Severity current separation: father	+51
8. Stability of home situation	−59
11. Proportion of caretaking in infancy: mother	−49
12. Proportion of caretaking in infancy: father	+47
18. Demands for good table manners	−55
30. Permissiveness for masturbation: mother	+60
32. Permissiveness for social sex play: mother	+52
37. Openness about sex: maternal grandparents	−52
43. Pressure for neatness and orderliness: father	−48
56. Demands for aggression toward peers: father	−50
112. Expectancy of sex differences in behavior: mother	−46
127. Reward of dependency: father	+60
164. Size of living space	+47
173. Nonpermissiveness factor score	−54

BOYS

13. Duration of breast feeding	+43
15. Severity of child's reaction to weaning	+54
16. Severity of weaning	+45
21. Amount of bed wetting now	+43
26. Reported amount of child's nudity: mother	+55
38. Sex anxiety: mother	−52
43. Pressure for neatness and orderliness: father	+46
105. Punishments for independence: father	−49
115. Reward for sex-appropriate behavior: father	−55
117. Expression of affection by child to father	−53
173. Nonpermissiveness factor score	−46

other forms of dependency is minimal for both sexes (Table 2), failing to replicate the Iowa findings. With respect to total observed antisocial aggression, however, the results are very similar to the earlier ones. For boys, the correlation with negative attention is .35, which is reduced to an insignificant .18 by partialling out activity level, while for girls, the partialling reduces the correlation only from .43 to .42. It seems evident that negative attention is a more integral part of the aggression system in girls than in boys, a conclusion that was reached on quite different grounds in the earlier study (Sears *et al.*, 1953, pp. 158–59). The low correlations with dependency, on the other hand, do not support the earlier suggestion that negative attention is more closely allied to dependency in boys than in girls. *Prosocial aggression,* which was not distinguished from *antisocial aggression* in the earlier research, shows no relation at all to negative attention.

Now as to antecedents. In the Iowa study, only one major contributor to negative attention was discovered. This was a mother interview scale measuring *amount of nurturance the mother gave when she was busy.* The relationship was negative; if she was nonresponsive to the child's supplications, he tended to develop the disruptive types of attention seeking defined as negative. This scale was not used in the present study, so the replicability of that finding cannot be tested. However, there were two 15-minute segments of the mother-child interaction which provided a comparison of "mother busy" with "mother attentive," as the stimulating conditions, and permitted measurement of the child's "bids for attention." The relevant data are given in Table 1. The last two lines in the table give the mean ratings, separately by sex, of the frequency and intensity of the child's efforts to secure attention under the two conditions. "Mother busy" elicited a significantly higher rating than "mother attentive." These ratings were made independently by two observers at every session and were based on reasonably objective definitions of "bidding" which, unfortunately, did not distinguish between negative and positive methods. No matter. There was almost no negative attention seeking during the "mother attentive" condition, when she was helping the child solve puzzles, and much of the excess of bidding for attention during the period in which the mother was filling out the questionnaire was definitely negative in type, especially toward the end of the period. Thus, while these data are not a reproduction of the Iowa data, they do show at the *action* if not the *learning* level that withdrawal or withholding of attention increases the amount of negative attention seeking.

A second major determinant of negative attention for both sexes appears to be a *general permissiveness and lack of standards or demands for mature behavior.* The evidence for this may be seen in the lists of scales given in Table 4, which include all the measures from the parent interviews and mother-child interaction situation that correlate with the observation measure of *negative attention seeking* at an .05 level of significance or better; for boys, an .05 level is indicated by correlation of .43, and for girls, .46.

There are two indications for this suggested relationship, one being the correlations with a factor analytic constructed score of mother's nonpermissiveness, the other the correlations with the various relevant individual scales used for scoring both the mother and the father interviews. The factor analytic score was derived from the summing of standard scores on 9 of the scales shown by Milton (1958) to have loadings of greater than .30 on the primary factor of *permissiveness-strictness*. A number of individual scales which are either components of the factor score, or at least congruent with that dimension, are also to be found in the lists.

In addition to the general permissiveness that seems evident in the reported treatment of both sexes, there are qualities of child rearing experience that seem to characterize the sexes differentially. For girls, there are several antecedent scales that refer to the father's behavior or attitudes. He looks to be an important person in the girl's life. For example, negative attention is associated with high father and low mother caretaking in infancy, with the degree of severity of current separation from the father, and with his rewarding of dependency. *His* permissiveness, as well as the mother's, is influential, too. In addition to these significantly correlated scales, there are several other father variables which are not included in the table because they are just below the .05 level: low use of ridicule, low use of modeling of good behavior, high satisfaction with the child's socialization, and high empathy for the child's feelings.

It looks as if these *negative attention seeking* little girls were "daddy's girls" from the begining; they formed a strong attachment to their fathers and separation from him produced an aggressive type of dependent supplication. Why aggressive? Because they had been masculinized by this emphasis on father-rearing. The picture is strikingly similar to that of twelve-year-old girls who have high aggression anxiety, as has been shown in a follow-up study of the *Patterns* children (Sears, 1961). An examination of the early socialized experiences of those girls revealed a strong emphasis on father caretaking in infancy and early childhood, and an exacerbation of aggression toward the parents at kindergarten age. They had apparently been treated more like boys than had most little girls, and their own aroused aggressive qualities created aggression anxiety for them. In the present group of girls, *negative attention seeking* is positively related (.43) to observed antisocial aggression in the nursery school and, more critically, is related −.47 to the total measure of feminine sex-typing. These were the *masculinized* girls.[2]

Although the father's role in this process is clear, the mother also is involved, for it is to be noted that negative attention is significantly related to her low expectation of sex differences in behavior at this age. When we discover that there is a correlation of −.43 with father's evaluation of mother, the state of affairs becomes a little clearer, perhaps. The father took over much of the child rearing because of his lack of confidence in the mother—or perhaps he expressed such low esteem as a justification for the fact that he *had* taken over!

We suggest the hypothesis that the parents of high *negative attention seeking* girls are somewhat slack in their pressures on their daughters, that the father lacks confidence in the mother's rearing activities and takes over a larger responsibility himself. This, coupled with the mother's lack of a feminizing attitude, masculinizes the little girl, and she behaves aggressively. At the same time, the infantilizing effect of low socialization demands leaves her relatively dependent in her reactions to others, and she combines the aggression and dependency into negative attention seeking. (Not surprisingly, the correlation with number of children in the family is −.43; there is little opportunity for correction by siblings!)

The picture for boys is less sharply defined, and though the

---

[2] Five separate measures of masculinity-femininity were obtained in the course of this research. The "total measure" was composed of the sum of the standard scores, calculated separately by sex of children, for these five measures (Sears, Alpert, and Rau, ms. in preparation).

effect of permissiveness is quite clearly indicated, there are two other parental elements that differ from those which are relevant to girls. First, there is a little cluster of early infant socialization measures. The high negative attention seekers were fed longer at the breast and were more severely weaned; these two measures are unrelated to one another in either sex, but in boys they are both significantly correlated with negative attention. There is a suggestion here of early socialization pressures.

A second point worth comment has to do with the father's influence. The high negative attention boys were described as showing little affection toward him, and he was characterized not only as permissive but also as neither expecting sex differences in behavior at this age ($r=-.42$) nor as rewarding masculine behavior when it occurred ($r=-.55$); since these latter two father scales are related to the extent of .69, they are evidently representing facets of the same quality. It looks as if the fathers of these high negative attention boys were *neglectful* of their sons rather than, as were the girls' fathers, *lovingly* permissive. There is no evidence that this treatment was destructive to the process of sex-typing, however, for negative attention and masculinity are only slightly negatively correlated in boys ($r=-.14$).

To summarize these findings in the form of an hypothesis, we suggest that negative attention seeking in boys is the product not only of general permissiveness by the mother, but also of severe infant socialization by the mother and a neglectfully permissive attitude toward the boy by the father, an attitude resulting in a low affectional attachment to him by his four-year-old son.

REASSURANCE

In view of the fact that the frequencies of reassurance and negative attention are entirely unrelated to one another in girls, and are even slightly negatively correlated in boys, it comes as no surprise to find that their antecedents are quite different. Again, too, there is a sharp difference in the apparent antecedents for boys and for girls.

Consider the girls first. Once more the father seems a salient figure. The mother's permissiveness is almost entirely unrelated

TABLE 5

Seeking Reassurance: Correlations with Parent Interview and Mother-Child Interaction Measures at Level $p < .05$

GIRLS

29. Parent's modesty: father	−57
64. Reasoning: use by mother	+52
84. Importance of teaching right and wrong: father's attitude	+49
116. Expression of affection by child toward mother	−60
133. Achievement standards: mother	+53
134. Achievement standards: father	+45
322. Mother's pressure for child's independence	+58
332. Mother's involvement in telephone game and enjoyment of it	+63

BOYS

18. Level of demands, table manners	+53
23. Permissiveness for going without clothes indoors: mother	−58
25. Pressure for modesty indoors: mother	+58
28. Parent's modesty: mother	+57
32. Permissive sex play among children: mother	−50
35. Giving sexual information to child—openness of mother's attitude	−55
38. Sex anxiety: mother	+61
51. Keeping track of child: mother	+49
167. Mother attitude scale: social sex play permissiveness	−44
173. Nonpermissiveness factor score	+67
322. Mother's pressure for child's independence	−66
326. Mother's directiveness	+49
330. Mother's warmth	−49

to the measure; only one sex permissiveness scale (indoor nudity) and one restrictiveness scale (house and furniture) have moderate correlations with it (.41 and −.44), and the nonpermissiveness factor score has almost none (−.15). But the father's sex behavior is strongly represented by his low modesty in the home (−.57), and (moderately) by high giving of sex information to the child (.41); these two father scales are correlated only −.26 with one another, so this suggests a fairly wide influence. It looks as if the father, in his open way, were presenting a rather strong sexual stimulus to the little girl. Why should this lead her to seek reassurance from others?

The answer seems reasonably straightforward if we assume that a child's sexual arousal by the parent of the opposite sex is an appropriate condition for creating a feeling of insecurity in her relationship with the same-sexed parent. This is essentially the rivalrous situation described by Freud as the Oedipus situation. Certainly in American culture there is ample opportunity for a girl to learn that sexual responsiveness to the parent of either sex is forbidden. If the father displays himself freely and also gives sexual information to the child, he is providing cue stimuli to arouse sexual impulses in her. There are certain consequences to be expected of this, of which the seeking of reassurance is only one, and perhaps a minor one at that. There should be a lack of affection—a remaining at arms length—with the mother, and the evidence for that is strong in the present instance; *seeking reassurance* is correlated –.60 with expression of affection toward the mother. There should be a general emotional sensitivity to deviation behavior, too, with emotional upset as the expression of guilt; we have strong evidence for this, but the data are too complicated to be added here and will have to be published in another place (Sears, Alpert, and Rau, ms. in preparation).

But lest the Oedipus explanation be given too ready credit for the full force of these relationships, consider the actual behavior of the mother herself. She is no lay figure standing idly by to be imbued with whatever projected hostilities her daughter may develop. She has qualities of her own that can contribute to the child's emotions. In this instance it is clear she does behave in ways calculated to increase her daughter's insecurity and to produce the "unaffectionateness" mentioned above. In the list are to be found her reported high standards of achievement (.53), and the the mother-child interaction, her pressure for the child to show independence (.58), her involvement in the telephone game, which was an achievement-oriented teaching task (.63); to these can be added the unlisted items of her rewarding of both achievement (.44) and adult role behavior (.44). To implement her efforts to secure productive, cooperative behavior from her daughter, she used reasoning (.52), was consistent in her care-taking policies (.42), and in the mother-child interaction she was judged to reward dependency (.39). She was persuasive rather than demanding, but her high standards would appear to give the proper setting for a certain contingency in giving her love.

The father was not only a sex object to the little girl, however. He was seen by her as the source of power in the family (.40), he felt it important to teach her the meaning of right and wrong (.49), and he, too, had high achievement standards (.45).

As an hypothesis, then, we suggest that the seeking for reas-surance by the little girl is a reaction to an insecurity aroused in her, especially with respect to her relations with her mother, by her father's sexual attractiveness and his moral and achieve-ment-oriented attitudes, and by her mother's own strong efforts to train her and hold her to high standards of achievement.

The apparent antecedents for the boy are similar in one respect, but strikingly different in another. Without exception, all the correlations that reach the .05 level of significance are with scales referring to the *mother,* that is, the parent of the oppo-site sex. But the mother-son relationship implied by the direc-tions of the correlations is just the opposite of the father-daughter relationship. The mother whose son seeks reassurance is cold, nonpermissive, anxious about both sex (.61) and aggression (.40), and has high conflict over the mother role (.40). She is one who keeps track of the child but does not necessarily do anything con-structive to train him; in the mother-child interaction she did not press for independence, nor reward it (−.41), nor did she even reward dependence (−.40).

This provides a picture of a relatively ineffectual mother, a conception supported, perhaps, by the father's low evaluation of her (−.40) and his tendency to interact with the child (.40).

With the boy, there is no sign that we can see of an Oedipus influence. On the contrary, the seeking of reassurance appears to be a product of persistent coldness and restrictiveness, perhaps even neglect, in the sense that rewarding of both dependence and independence is avoided.

BEING NEAR

This is one of the two "immature" (or passive or physical) forms of positive dependency behavior. It is characterized by the child's efforts to get close to another child or to the teacher, and to remain there without necessarily engaging in verbal contact.

Among the *girls*, there was a close correlation with the other immature form, *touching and holding*, and a moderately close

TABLE 6

Being Near: Correlations with Parent Interview and Mother-Child Interaction Measures at Level $p < .05$

GIRLS

1. Age of child	−46
16. Severity of weaning, summary scale	−50
32. Permissiveness, sex play among children: mother	+50
35. Giving sexual information to child—openness of mother's attitude	+48
38. Sex anxiety: mother	−46
43. Pressure for neatness and orderliness: father	−47
53. Overt expression of aggression in home: mother	−54
103. Rewarding of independence: father	−47
137. Influence on child: mother	+55
145. Caretaking consistency: mother	+54
342. Mother's punishment of child's aggression	+46

BOYS

24. Permissiveness for going without clothes indoors: father	−45
48. Expect child to take responsibility: mother	−59
51. Keeping track of child: mother	+50
80. Sex-stereotyping of parents' roles: father	+43
86. Models of good behavior: father	−48
135. Resemblance to mother	−44
153. Mother's evaluation of father	−45
155. Maternal grandparents discipline	−46
170. Child behavior scale: maturity	−44
171. Winterbottom scale: mean age of expected independence	+68
330. Mother's warmth	−54

one with *negative attention seeking.* There is a noticeable similarity to the latter in the antecedents that reach an .05 level of significance, especially those that imply a permissive treatment with low demands and expectations for mature behavior. However, while the father's low demands are in evidence, there is one important difference between this list and the one for negative attention: there is no indication here of an especially close relationship to the father.

For *boys,* the correlates of *being near* do not reflect the maternal permissiveness, seen in the girls, although there is some indication of a similar tendency toward infantilization. While there is no relation to age ($r=-.11$), there is a significant negative correlation with maturity as evaluated by the mother on a semi-objective check list of skills the child has attained. This measure is in itself related only moderately to chronological age ($r=.34$), but it correlates $-.41$ with keeping track of the child, that is, mothers who keep track most vigilantly rate their sons as less mature. This high keeping-track measure, together with the low pressure for neatness and orderliness, are both significantly associated with *being near,* and hence we suggest that these low demand and high supervision behaviors by the mother may tend to infantilize the boy, and this is exhibited not only by the mother's judgment of his maturity level but by the high occurrence of *being near* as a form of dependency toward other children and teachers.

The role of the father in this connection is interesting. He appears prominently among the associated measures, not only in his nonpermissiveness with respect to indoor nudity but as a reporter of a clear stereotyping of masculine role for himself; he makes the distinction strongly between the sex roles of the parents. Wives whose husbands do this do not evaluate their husbands highly ($r=-.64$), and hence it is to be expected that these boys who score high on *being near* have fathers who receive low evaluation from their wives. There is also an almost significant correlation ($r=.42$) with a measure of discrepancy between the two parents' child-rearing attitudes. These relationships suggest that the father may be rather ineffectual in his child rearing because he lacks the confidence of the mother and operates in opposition to her. Her slackness in pressing for more maturity, then, becomes a significant determinant of the boys' low level of maturity as exhibited in high use of *being near*. One might speculate further that the initial disagreement between the parents may have retarded the child's maturity because of the uncertainty of what behavior would or would not be rewarded, and that the mother's infantilizing treatment may have been a result, rather than a cause, of the slow development. There is no way to test this notion within the present body of data, however.

TOUCHING AND HOLDING

This is the other category of "immature" dependency behavior. Since it correlates strongly with *being near,* in girls, it is not sur-

TABLE 7

Touching and Holding: Correlations with Parent Interview and Mother-Child Interaction Measures at Level $p < .05$

GIRLS	
16. Severity of weaning	−46
53. Overt expression of aggression by mother	−58
115. Reward of sex-appropriate behavior: father	−50
172. Winterbottom scale: number of items	+50
BOYS	
2. Correspondence between m-c interaction and child's behavior at home	−43
41. Restrictions: house and furniture: father	−44
63. Aggression anxiety: father	−48
90. Expectancy of conscience: mother	−45
97. Tangible reward: father	−58
99. High psychological vs. tangible reward: father	+58
112. Expectancy of sex differences in behavior: mother	−46
123. Dependency on father	+58
142. Severity of current separation-status from mother	+51
156. Paternal grandparents' discipline	−57
163. Number of children in family	+47
352. Child's willingness to adopt deviant child role in telephone game	+51
359. Mother's pressure and reward for adult role behavior	−50
368. Mother's use of models with child	−54

prising to find considerable similarity in the associated antecedent scales, although several of those which reach significance at the .05 level with *being near* fail to reach that level in correlation with *touching and holding.*

For *boys,* the correlation of these two dependency measures is much lower, .16, and hence it is not surprising to find no overlap whatever between the two lists of antecedent scales. It is difficult to gain any very clear picture of the training or instigating conditions. The facilitating effect of current separation from the mother is matched by just the opposite effect of separation from the father ($r=.38$), although the boy is described as dependent on the father in the interview ($r=.58$). The father appears to be an unanxious and undemanding person, and the mother is much the same. Again, as with *being near,* there is the atmosphere of infantilization.

POSITIVE ATTENTION

This is the more "mature" (or verbal or active) form of dependency behavior, although there is no correlation with either chronological age, in our relatively narrow age group, or the mother's objective estimates of maturity. It is a verbal form of dependency primarily, and involves efforts to secure approval of others. In girls, it shows a zero relation with *negative attention seeking* and the two "immature" positive forms of dependency, but it is positively related to *seeking reassurance.*

As for child rearing antecedents, again we find an emphasis on sex permissiveness of the mother, together with low proportional caretaking by the mother during infancy and high separation from her currently. The mother rewards the girl for dependency and sees her as resembling the mother herself. She expresses affection toward the child ($r=.42$), and so does the father ($r=.45$). This permissiveness concerning sex and dependency does not extend to aggression, however, for both the parents are strict on that score. The net impression is of a mother who is affectionate, tolerant of sex and dependent behavior, restrictive with respect to aggression and sees the little girl as an extension of herself—but who never has spent a great deal of time with her, relatively speaking. From a learning and action standpoint, these

TABLE 8

Positive Attention: Correlations with Parent Interview and Mother-Child Interaction Measures at Level *p* < .05

GIRLS

11. Proportional amount of caretaking in infancy by mother	–62
28. Parent's modesty: mother	–48
33. Sexuality in child: mother's report	+54
37. Openness about sex: mother's parents	–51
58. Permissiveness for aggression toward parents: mother	–49
61. Punishment for aggression against parents: father	+48
126. Rewarding of dependency: mother	+50
128. Punishment of dependency: mother	–63
135. Resemblance to mother	+63
138. Directiveness: mother	–46
142. Severity of current separation-status from mother	+53

BOYS

4. Tension re m-c interaction	–49
12. Amount of caretaking in infancy by father	–49
27. Amount of social nudity practiced by child: father's report	–45
39. Sex anxiety: father	+50
60. Punishment for aggression against parents: mother	+54
111. Imitation of parents	+52
152. Extent to which child is acquainted with father's work and activities outside the home	–52

behaviors add up to high reinforcement and also high interference, a combination from which the highest amount of dependency behavior would be expected.

So far as boys are concerned, *positive attention seeking* has a small positive correlation with *negative attention* and a tiny negative relation to the "immature" forms of dependency.

On the antecedent side, information is sparse. Again we see the low proportion of infant caretaking by the same sexed parent, but in this instance this behavior is associated with high sex anxiety (low permissiveness) on the father's part rather than high permissiveness. As with girls, however, the mother is nonpermissive of aggression. The boy is believed to be very little acquainted with the father's work, also. This combination of scales on the antecedent side (low permissiveness for sex and aggression) might seem to suggest a feminizing process, but the correlation of *positive attention* with a measure of *masculinity* is only –.14, so clearly we cannot conclude that positive attention is a bit of feminine behavior brought on entirely by the same experiences that produce a nonmasculine sex typing.

It is interesting to note that the boy who shows high positive attention is said by the parents to imitate them a lot, which suggests an interpretation of positive attention as a maturity-seeking kind of behavior on the child's part. In view of the strict parental control of both sex and aggression, the status of being a child probably has little to recommend it to the boy, and positive attention serves to bring him into a more favorable relationship with the parents. Its more mature quality, perhaps because of its emphasis on verbal interchange, is no doubt reassuring for parents who dislike open sexual and aggressive behavior.

In this connection, a special comment should be made about the two parent interview scales referring to proportional amount of caretaking in infancy. As can be seen from the Table 9, these scales are negatively correlated with sex anxiety in *both* parents of boys. That is, the fathers and mothers who were judged to have high sex anxiety tended to avoid caretaking of the infant boy. There was little relation between these variables in either parent of girl babies. It looks as if the boy represented more of a sex symbol to both parents, and if they had high sex anxiety, they

TABLE 9

Correlations Between Parents' Sex Anxiety and Proportional Amount of Infant Caretaking

Interview Scale	Boys' Parents		Girls' Parents	
	Mother Sex Anxiety	Father Sex Anxiety	Mother Sex Anxiety	Father Sex Anxiety
Caretaking: mother	–46	–07	00	00
Caretaking: father	18	–45	–30	–09

tended to avoid caretaking. When one considers that holding, feeding, and diaper changing are the major *required* functions of the infant caretaker, this avoidance is understandable.

These relationships make clearer what is implied by the low caretaking of the same sexed parent. The girls were treated to low caretaking by the mother, but not because, in any consistent way, she had high sex anxiety. This low caretaking occurred *independently* of the mother's feelings about sex. Caretaking thus gains clear status as a relevant antecedent variable in its own right and not as a correlate of the sex permissiveness syndrome. In boys, however, the low father caretaking is just part and parcel of the general nonpermissiveness and anxiety about sex that are the associates of high positive attention seeking.

We propose the following interpretation and hypotheses. First, that the absolute amount of caretaking was sufficient for all these children, of both sexes, to have established both an affection for and a dependent interaction system with the parents. Second, that for the girl, low maternal caretaking represented a withholding of full satisfaction of this dependency interaction; coupled with strictness on the expression of aggression and high current separation, it forced the girl to unusual efforts to please and attract the mother in a mature and feminine way. If we may take the mother's estimate of how much the little girl resembled her as, at least, in part, a measure of the mother's goal, then evidently *positive attention seeking* was associated (.63) with the mother's satisfaction. Thus, third, the girls' *positive attention seeking* represents a successful reaction to a long-term frustration (in the form of contingent love response).

The first step in our reasoning about the boy is the same as that about the girls, but the second is different. Low caretaking by the father is interpreted as part of the more general picture of rejection which is reflected also in the judgment that the boy at preschool age had little acquaintance with his father's work outside the home. These two father scales have no relation to one another (.10), and hence represent different measures of the rejection. Father rejection, coupled with the mother's strictness concerning aggression, add up to continuous frustration *without* the guidance toward social progression provided for the girls by their mothers' permissiveness with respect to sex and dependency. Thus, third, the boys' *positive attention seeking* is also interpreted as a response to long-term frustration, but the lack of an associated "invitation to dependency" leaves them free to develop other responses (autonomy, avoidance, independence) to signals of impending nurturance.

There is a slight confirmation of these hypotheses, but only slight. For both sexes there was a small positive correlation (girls=.23; boys=.27) between *positive attention seeking* and the number of bids for attention elicited by the "mother busy" situation in the mother-child interaction; the "withholding" stimulation was effective. But when the "mother attentive" situation was presented, the correlation for girls was +.62 and that for boys was −.32; when attention was actually offered, the girls grabbed for it, while the boys rejected it. With respect to *independence* shown during all four sections of the interaction, girls showed little or no relation to *positive attention seeking* (.18) while the correlation for boys was significant at the .05 level (.44). This *independent* behavior is perhaps one of the alternatives learned by the boy in the relative absence of the conditions for dependency provided by permissiveness, reward and low punishment.

DISCUSSION

From a general theory of learning, one would expect that those behaviors of the child which led to most frequent reinforcement by parental responses would be most strongly established. Clinical observation and psychoanalytic theory have long emphasized the importance of early oral activity, or the oral stage, as playing an important part of the development of dependent qualities. Feeding and caretaking—the *giving* of rewards—are predominant parental activities during the first 12 to 18 months of the child's life. During this period he is essentially passive and recipient, so far as food and loving handling are concerned. He presumably learns to expect care, and his operant behaviors that immediately precede gratification become strengthened. If a dependency *drive* is formed by these experiences, it should instigate behavior that would lead to a resumption of his passivity and to the securing of rewards from the parents. *If* a drive existed as a continuous instigator, one would anticipate that new actions would gradually develop as the child's motoric and perceptual capacities matured and as his increasing age and status stimulated new expectancies of him by his parents. Such behaviors as being near, touching and holding, and eventually the verbal seeking of reassurance, comfort and positive attention, should replace the smiling, arching, mouthing, and passive offering of his body for caresses and holding that compose his first repertoire of dependency supplications.

In an effort to test the hypothesis that oral or other caretaking experiences establish dependency response strength, we compared the frequency of occurance of our five observation categories with three measures of oral experience that seemed to be possible antecedents. The reasoning was that high reinforcement would create the equivalent of fixation and that later dependency behavior would be more frequent as a result. There was no evidence whatever to support the hypothesis, nor did the rather small obtained antecedent-consequent relationships replicate those found in the Iowa study. The crudity and inexactness of the antecedent measures make us hesitate to consider this failure crucial to the theory, but it is worth reporting in order to discourage others from wasting time on this method of examining what is in fact a very complex theory and at present a very poorly defined one.

The second and third hypotheses must be considered together. These are that (1) continuing permissiveness for sexual and dependent behavior, and (2) frustration through the withholding of love and affection, will serve as reinforcers of dependency behavior. The permissiveness hypothesis is direct; the more opportunity the child is given for practice, and the more frequent reward he receives, the stronger the responses will become. The frustration hypothesis is more complex. Coldness and nonpermissiveness are conditions that might be expected to operate in the opposite way. In fact, of course, these withholdings of reward are only relative, not in any conceivable sense complete, and hence may be presumed to provide the quality of aperiodic intermittent reinforcement. Thus, the child with a nonpermissive and nonrewarding father has fewer opportunities to receive rewarded

practice of his dependency responses; but what he does receive
is scheduled in such a way as to increase the strength of the
operant reponses.

So far as girls are concerned, the permissiveness hypothesis
receives quite clear support in connection with all the categories
of dependency. The frustration hypothesis is supported, also,
with respect to *seeking positive attention*. For boys, there is no
support for the permissiveness principle but there is for the frus-
tration. This latter conclusion rests on our interpretation of the
mother's coldness and slack standards and the father's sex *non-
permissiveness* as frustrations.

Basically, then, the second and third hypotheses gain support
from the data. The sex differences in the variables that have
proved relevant, however, and the lack of clear intercorrelational
evidence for a single trait of dependency, suggest that the rela-
tionships between child rearing and the several types of depend-
ent behavior are more complicated than these hypotheses have
implied.

The positive relation of maternal sex and dependency per-
missiveness with four of the girls' dependency measures, and the
negative relation of paternal sex permissiveness with three of
the boys', suggest a possible difference in the reinforcement con-
ditions for the two sexes. Dependency, sociability, verbal respon-
siveness to the mother—all represented by *positive attention seek-
ing*—appear to be associated with the mother's satisfaction with
her daughter; these are appropriate for the sex typing of the girl.
Thus, dependency seems to be acceptable or even desired, and
mothers who encourage intimacy achieve their aims. For boys,
however, the various forms of dependency seem to be associated
with coldness in the mother, slackness of standards, and a rejec-
tion of intimacy by the father. It is as if the dependency suppli-
cations were efforts to overcome indifference and neglect, as if
they represented reactions to some kind of insecurity stemming
from withdrawal or withholding of parental affection. Thus,
the same overt behavior may be interpreted as *progressive* in
girls and *regressive* in boys.

SUMMARY

The higher average intercorrelation for girls than for boys, among the various subcategories of dependency, is reflected in the greater similarity among the five lists of correlated antecedent scales. There is a consistent theme of *permissiveness with respect to sex and dependency* running through four of the five girls' lists. The differentiating variables that appear to produce one subcategory rather than another are mainly three: (1) the role played by the father, (2) the severity of demands for mature conduct placed on the little girl, and (3) the severity of aggression control. In other words, high sex and dependency permissiveness seem to provide the basic dependency motivation—or behavior quality— while the forms of expression are determined by these other three types of influence. *Negative attention* was the product of low demands and restrictions plus the intimate intrusion of the father into the child-rearing process; *reassurance* was the product of high demands for achievement coupled with sex anxiety created for the little girl by her father's role as a sexually stimulating male; *being near* and *touching and holding* were the products of low demands, but without the masculinizing entrance of the father that created *negative attention seeking; positive attention* was produced by a nonpermissive and punitive attitude toward aggression.

From both a learning and an action standpoint, then, the data on girls' dependency seem to be in accord with theoretical principles derived from experimental studies. Permissiveness for and reward of dependency have a reinforcing effect; the permissiveness provides opportunity for practice, and reward specifies the reinforcing state of affairs following operant activity. Permissiveness for sex behavior represents the conditions, also, that are needed for making dependent responses, for all the varieties except negative attention (and even some instances of that) involve approaches to another person, either physical or verbal. The seeking of closeness, of intimacy, can be either dependent or sexual, and is probably usually both in the little girl. If the mother is not free of sex anxiety, these approaches could be threatening to her own defenses and discomforting to her sense of the proprieties of interpersonal relationships. Thus, sex permissiveness may be considered a measure of the broad range of opportunities for practice. Finally, the severity of current separation from the mother represents a measure of interference with the dyadic interaction, and offers the appropriate circumstances for facilitation of the operant activity.

A comparable analysis of *boys'* dependency is by no means so easy, and for good reason. The virtual lack of intercorrelation among the five subcategories has raised a serious question as to whether one can justify ascribing any such *generalization* to summarize them. Certainly, a review of the five lists heretofore presented does not reveal any common element comparable to the sex permissiveness in the socialization of girls. If there is any one reasonably widespread relationship, it is with *sex nonpermissiveness* of one or both parents, although this does not apply to *negative attention,* which is associated with high permissiveness as in girls. With this exception, however, there is some suggestion of a theme running through the antecedents for the remaining subcategories. This is a rather vague representation of an *inhibited and ineffectual mother*—and to some extent *father,* too—who provides little freedom for the boy, and little incentive for rapid maturing.

The difference between the boy and girl antecedents is very striking, even though our description of the pattern for boys suffers a certain inexactness. The girls appear to be learning to be dependent as a normal progressive aspect of their socialization; the child rearing conditions are what would be expected in the circumstances. For the boys, however, if our interpretations are correct, there is a theme of nonsupport for such learning; it is as if dependency for them was a *regressive* rather than *progressive* form of response, a reaction to chronic frustration.

In summary, then, the major cluster of antecedents for the various measures of girls' nursery school dependency are those involving maternal permissiveness for sex and dependency. These are present in some degree for all but one of the subcategories. The special antecedents related to each of the subcategories include:

(1) For *negative attention seeking,* low demands and restrictions, plus the high participation of the father in the girl's child rearing.

(2) For *seeking reassurance,* high demands for achievement from both parents, plus an apparent sex anxiety produced by the father's sex permissiveness.

(3) For *being near* and *touching* and *holding,* low demands and restrictions without the masculinizing entrance of the father into the girls' rearing.

(4) For *positive attention seeking,* low maternal caretaking in infancy, as well as currently, and a nonpermissive attitude toward aggression.

The parental variables correlated with boys' dependency were generally ones implying coldness, slackness of standards, and neglect by the mother, without any real permissiveness, and a generally nonpermissive attitude—especially about sex—by the father. The one definite exception to this statement relates to *negative attention seeking,* which in boys, as in girls, was associated with maternal sex permissiveness; there was an additional special cluster of variables for boys that implied early severity of socialization.

The only detectable special variables relevant to the other subcategories were as follows: (1) for *touching and holding,* some unspecified influence of the father; (2) for *positive attention seeking,* low father participation and strictness of aggression control by the mother.

REFERENCES

Dollard, J., Doob, L. W., Miller, N. E., Mowrer, O. H., & Sears, R. R. *Frustration and aggression.* New Haven: Yale Univ. Press, 1939.

Gewirtz, J. L. A learning analysis of the effects of normal stimulation, privation, and deprivation on the acquisition of social motivation and attachment. In B. M. Foss (Ed.). *Determinants of infant behavior.* New York: Wiley, 1961.

Heathers, G. L. Emotional dependence and independence in nursery school play. *J. genet. Psychol.,* 1955, **87**, 37–57.

Milton, G. A. A factor analytic study of child-rearing behaviors. *Child Developm.,* 1958, 29, 382–392.

Murray, Jr., H. A. *Explorations in personality.* New York: Oxford Univ. Press, 1938.

Sears, R. R. Relation of early socialization experiences to aggression in middle childhood. *J. abn. soc. Psychol.,* 1961, 63, 466–492.

Sears, R. R., Alpert, R., & Rau, L. *Identification and child rearing,* in preparation.

Sears, R. R., Maccoby, E. E., & Levin, H. *Patterns of child rearing.* Evanston, Ill.: Row, Peterson, 1957.

Sears, R. R., Whiting, J. W. M., Nowlis, V., & Sears, P. S. Some child-rearing antecedents of aggression and dependency in young children. *Genet. Psychol. Monogr.,* 1953, 47, 135–234.

Whiting, J. W. M. The frustration complex in Kwoma society. *Man,* 1944, 115, 140–144.

Some Reflections on the Law of Effect Produce a New Alternative to Drive Reduction

NEAL E. MILLER

Yale University

I HAVE frequently said that the betting odds are against the correctness of the strong form of the drive-reduction hypothesis of reinforcement (e.g., Miller, 1957; 1959, p. 257). But the only way to emphasize that I am not completely committed to this hypothesis is to try to formulate an alternative one. In this paper I shall take a tentative fling at such a formulation. I shall not present it in finished form, partly because I do not have time, and partly because it seems wise to leave many alternatives open to be narrowed down by further experimental work.

Formulating a different hypothesis does not mean, however, that I shall stop answering those objections to the drive-reduction hypothesis that are falacious, or stop designing experiments suggested by this fruitful hypothesis. There is nothing to prevent a scientist from exploring simultaneously a number of different hypotheses.

Before trying my own new formulation, I shall examine various theories of reinforcement, point out some of the chief difficulties they encounter, and outline a few experiments suggested by such an examination. Some of these experiments seem interesting in their own right; if they also help to narrow down the range of possibilities confronting the theorist who is wrest-

NOTE: Some of the research reported in this paper was supported by USPHS Grants MY647 and MY2949 from the National Institute of Mental Health, United States Public Health Service, Bethesda, Maryland. I want to thank Dr. Frank A. Logan and Dr. Allan R. Wagner for reading the manuscript and making helpful suggestions in spite of the fact that the time allowed by the deadline was extremely brief.

ling with the problem of reinforcement, that will be an additional value.

In evaluating various hypotheses concerning reinforcement, one should bear in mind three points which can be extracted from the history of science, as expounded, for example, by Conant (1947). First, a theory may be fruitful, leading to valuable research, even though it eventually is proven to be wrong, or indeed because it is formulated specifically enough so that it can be disproven. Second, a given piece of evidence which seems to disprove an otherwise useful theory may be based upon a misconception, as when, for example, the opponents of the oxygen theory of combustion confused the two different gases, hydrogen and carbon monoxide. Third, a useful theory is never abandoned because of contradictory evidence, but is overthrown only by a superior one.

Mere Frequency Inadequate

The honored first place should be given to a dead hypothesis, namely, that frequency alone determines what is learned, as though by wearing a path in the nervous system from sheer use. It is an unfortunate commentary on our progress in this particular area to date that we cannot do homage to other honorably dead hypotheses. In fact, a survey leaves us with the impression that the situation is something like that for the treatment of the common cold—there are a multitude of prescriptions because none is satisfactory.

The frequency hypothesis is dead because learning can involve the replacement of a frequent response by one that is extremely infrequent at first, and hence ought to fall progressively further behind if repetition were all that counted (Tolman, 1932). Furthermore, the repetition of a response without reinforcement leads to experimental extinction instead of additional strengthening. Clearly, something in addition to mere frequency is required.

EMPIRICAL LAW OF EFFECT

Out of the myriad possibilities for learned associations, rewards seem to determine what actually is learned, or at least what actually is performed.[1] Some of the most valuable work on learning has been done by using events that clearly are rewarding without being concerned with the reasons why they are rewarding. Such work has discovered significant variables that influence the effectiveness of a reward, to mention only a few, the gradient of reinforcement, effects of various schedules of reward, and effects of various types of correlation between dimensions of response and dimensions of reward. On the basis of data gathered in this way, mathematical models of learning have been developed.[2]

Other developments have involved starting with empirical principles of reinforcement determined in simple situations, applying these principles to somewhat more complicated situations, deducing outcomes, and then testing these deductions. My own work on conflict behavior (Miller, 1944; 1959; 1961a), social learning and imitation (Miller and Dollard, 1941), personality and psychotherapy (Dollard and Miller, 1950; Miller, 1963b), and graphic communication and education (Miller, et al, 1957) falls into this category. Many other people have done similar work; this approach has been and will continue to be fruitful.

At the simplest level, which is where most of us work most of the time, we use only a few clear-cut rewards, such as giving food to a hungry animal or letting an electrically shocked animal escape. We know very well from experience that these rewards work, at least in the laboratory situations in which we use them, and give the matter very little further thought.

When we want to get theoretically elegant, we say that our

[1] For a discussion of the relationship of motivation to learning see Miller (1959 pp. 259–260) and note that the traditional experiments on the learning-performance distinction greatly underestimate the practical importance of motivation by trying to rule out some of the main ways (e.g., causing S to expose himself to and pay attention to cues, eliciting responses, etc.) in which drive and reward affect learning.

[2] Although Estes (1950) sometimes assumes the mantle of a pure contiguity theorist in order to lure followers to read his mathematics, a close examination shows that he uses the empirical law of effect by assuming that he is dealing with a situation which establishes connections (or with one that disconnects them) on the basis of what he knows will happen in the situation, rather than on the basis of a detailed theoretical analysis from which he deduces the formation or breaking of connections.

procedure is not completely circular because we use the learning of one response to determine that an experimental operation is rewarding and then *assume* that it will be rewarding for all other responses that are learnable (Miller and Dollard, 1941, p. 30; Meehl, 1950). Thus, although someone using the empirical law of effect has to have a long catalogue of rewarding versus neutral situations, he need not have an impossibly long catalogue listing the effects of situations separately for different kinds of learnable responses.

The Pain-Fear Paradox

We have not bothered to test carefully the truth of the foregoing crucial assumption that allows us to shorten the catalogue. In fact, there is a good chance that it is not true!

If one considers fear to be a response because it can be learned, then rewarding a hungry animal which has learned to fear a buzzer by giving him food immediately after the buzzer has elicited the fear, probably will not strengthen the fear but will weaken it by counterconditioning. I say probably because this situation has not been studied experimentally as carefully as it should be in view of its importance for various theories of reinforcement, and its practical importance for psychotherapy (Miller, 1963b).

Our common escape from this dilemma is to say that the food elicits and reinforces a response that is incompatible with fear. Perhaps this is satisfactory, but perhaps it is not. Can we find a reward, such as electrical stimulation of the brain in a certain location, the administration of which to a frightened animal will not immediately tend to reduce symptoms of fear? If so, can this reward be used to strengthen fear?

Let us look more closely at the role of incompatibility. When a rat is rewarded for pressing a bar, the response of ducking down to the food dish elicited by the food is incompatible with that of standing up to press the bar. Indeed, the anticipatory ducking responses do sometimes obviously intrude and interfere with pressing the bar.[3] But if we are hard-headed about it and

---

[3] See a sound motion picture film, Miller and Hart (1948).

deliver the food only if the animal first has pressed the bar, he forms a sequential discrimination and learns to press the bar before ducking to the food dish. In this case, the obvious physical incompatibility does not prevent learning!

If we had a method of recording fear, moment by moment, and were strict about giving the food only when the buzzer elicited fear, could we succeed in strengthening fear by rewarding it with food?

Now let us look at the other side of the problem. Something about pain serves to reinforce fear, as demonstrated by the fact that pain can be used to establish fear of a neutral stimulus. But this same something does not seem to serve to reinforce other responses immediately preceding pain. Why? Let us call this the pain-fear paradox.

Again, our escape is to say that the pain elicits incompatible responses which are reinforced by the termination of pain. In this case we do not have to wait for some measure of fear; we can proceed immediately to make electric shock contingent upon pressing a bar. But we already know that this procedure does not reinforce pressing the bar; it teaches the animal to stop pressing.

Incidentally, this same observation causes trouble also for a hedonic interpretation of reward. If an electric shock reinforces the learning of fear, it must be pleasant and hence should reward learning to press the bar. Of course this sounds absurd. But how can a hypothesis that pleasant satisfiers strengthen and unpleasant annoyers weaken responses explain the apparent dual effects of pain, strengthening fear but failing to strengthen pressing the bar?

Now you may feel that there must be some difference between the responses incompatible with bar pressing elicited by the food in the dish and those elicited by the electric shock on the grid, and that such a difference will allow us to escape from the dilemma I am posing. Indeed, you may be right, but I hope that I have convinced you that we may just possibly have been overlooking a real problem worthy of additional study by allowing our intuition about what certainly would happen to make the explanation in terms of incompatible responses more impressive than it should be in its simplest, most obvious, form.

Let me stir up a bit of further thought by proposing an experiment which I had hoped to have completed before I came, but did not even get the time to start. This delay will allow you to make your own predictions, which I hope to test.

Recently, Fowler and I (1963) used the fact that giving rats a shock on their hind-feet just as they touch food causes them to lurch forward. The response of lurching forward would not be expected to be incompatible with running; in fact it should summate with running. And, with the currents used, shocked rats did run down the alley faster than nonshocked ones, being speeded up more by stronger shocks, and also accelerating more than nonshocked ones as they neared the goal. This looks pretty good for the hypothesis that the slowing down often observed when animals are shocked at the goal is due to the shock ordinarily eliciting responses that are incompatible with running. Perhaps, when incompatible responses are eliminated, a painful shock actually will reinforce responses of approach as well as of fear.

The experiment I propose uses a Y-maze with two very distinctive arms. Rats will receive food and shock to the hind-feet at the end of one arm and only food at the end of the other. A combination of free and forced trials will insure that they run down both arms an equal number of times. If they learn to run down the shock arm faster, as might be expected from the results which Fowler and I secured, it will be hard to say that the shock elicits responses incompatible with running. How can one say that the shock elicits incompatible responses, if it actually speeds up the running? But on the free-choice trials will the rats choose the shock arm?

Choice of the shock arm in my proposed experiment would allow the empirical law of effect to escape complete circularity and thus to shorten its catalogue from impossibly long, to merely very long. It would also save the hedonic hypothesis from the dilemma of two opposite effects from pain. But many of you might be unwilling to take the logically required step of treating pain as a satisfier because it strengthens responses. As we shall see later, this outcome would also be good for the optimum-level hypothesis and for Sheffield's drive-induction hypothesis. By the same token, choice of the nonshock side would be embarrassing for all of these hypotheses.

Returning to the empirical law of effect, it is rather unsatisfactory to have three long empirical lists of situations, the onset of which is rewarding, the termination of which is rewarding, and those which seem to be neutral. This, of course, is what has caused theorists to look for some feature common to the events in a given list in order to reduce the catalogue of rewards to a more parsimonious description. It is a fascinating, but tantalizing, puzzle. Let us now briefly review some of the principle hypotheses.

The Hedonic Hypothesis

We have already mentioned this hypothesis. For the subjective words, pleasure and pain, Thorndike (1913) has attempted to substitute the more objective words, satisfying and annoying. But Thorndike's objective definitions of satisfying and annoying are in terms of exactly the types of behavior that would be expected on the basis of their presumed reinforcing effect, namely, seeking and doing nothing to avoid, or avoiding and doing nothing to seek. If one adds the necessary neutral category, one can see that there really is no advance over the catalog involved in the empirical law of effect, unless one can get some relatively independent, objective criterion for classifying events as satisfying or annoying.

Not so long ago, Delgado, Roberts, and I (1954) showed that stimulation of certain areas of the brain had all the functional characteristics of an annoying stimulus such as pain or fear. Very shortly thereafter, Olds and Milner (1954) showed that stimulating other areas had all the functional characteristics of a satisfier, or reward.[4] These discoveries have revived, somewhat,

---

[4] I mention the sequence of these discoveries to correct a curious bit of historical fantasy in a recent, widely read book by Mowrer (1960a, p. 209) which refers to studies by Olds and Milner (1954) and then goes on to say: "Inspired by the work of the investigators cited, N. E. Miller (1957) has recently reported the localization of a *distress* or 'alarm' center in the cat brain, stimulation of which operates precisely as does the onset of strong peripheral drive or 'punishment'."

the attractiveness of the hedonic hypothesis. What are the ana-
tomical, biochemical, electrophysiological, or other characteristics
which differentiate these two types of central stimulation from
each other, and from neutral stimulation? I shall leave that
question for my two distinguished colleagues within whose field
it rightfully falls. But if there are indeed identifiable reward and
aversion systems that can be reliably differentiated by anatomical
or physiological techniques, we have advanced a long step toward
the solution of our problem, although we may still be troubled by
the pain-fear dilemma.

THE DRIVE-REDUCTION HYPOTHESIS

One notices that a reduction in annoying stimulation acts
as a reward. One also observes that many of the satisfying stimuli,
such as food to a hungry animal, or water to a thirsty one, have
the effect of eventually reducing their drives to zero, after which
the goal substance loses its reward value. Thus, by assuming
that the hunger or thirst drives are an aversive stimulus, one has
the tempting possibility of reducing the two factors involved in
the hedonic hypothesis to one. To put it another way, upon
observing that the operations for producing satiation are cor-
related with those for producing reward, one assumes that the
process of satiation causes the reward.

This hypothesis immediately runs against intuitive judg-
ment which says that it is the pleasant stimulation, rather than
the relief from pain, that one seeks in food and drink, and espe-
cially in sex. But conceivably it is a matter of the relation of
onset to offset. If someone steps on your toe, you say, "Get off,
that hurts!" But if you have been wearing a pair of tight shoes
on a long day's hike, you may experience a thrill of joy and say,
"My, but it feels good to take off those shoes!"

The results on cats were presented in a film "Learning Motivated by
Electrical Stimulation of the Brain" as part of my address as President of
Division 3 at the 1953 meetings of the American Psychological Association;
were presented to the Fourteenth International Congress of Psychology in
June (Miller, 1954); and were finally published in full detail (Delgado,
Roberts and Miller, 1954). The 1957 article cited by Mowrer refers to the
latter publication, as well as to the 1953 presentation.

It is essential to distinguish between drive and need because certain needs, such as deficiency of oxygen or the need to escape carbon monoxide, produce no drive. Or one may note that all stimuli seem to become aversive if intense enough, and advance the hypothesis that the reduction in intense stimulation is the basis for reinforcement (Miller and Dollard, 1941). For the moment we are concerned with the strong form of the hypothesis, which says that all reinforcement is produced by the reduction of strong stimulation.

Sheffield and Roby (1950) have shown that saccharine can serve as a reward. From the fact that it is non-nutritive they assume that it does not reduce hunger. In testing this assumption, my students and I have found that prefeeding a hungry animal with saccharine will reduce the subsequent consumption of sucrose solution, milk, lab chow, or corn oil, while saccharine given by mouth reduces subsequent consumption, given via stomach fistula it does not (Miller, 1957). Such research is interesting in its own right and tends to convert an argument against the drive-reduction hypothesis into evidence for it. Furthermore, Smith and Capretta (1956) have observed that feeding with saccharine seems to protect rats from insulin convulsions, which suggests to me an experiment on the effects of the sweet taste of saccharine on the level of blood sugar.

On the other hand, when I tried to rule out a possible depressing effect on the taste endings by tests involving bar pressing during extinction, prefeeding by saccharine only produced a statistically reliable effect when the amounts were so large that one could suspect the animals of becoming waterlogged.

Similar experiments by Sheffield, Wulff, and Backer (1951) on sex involved the assumption that this is a unitary drive which is reduced only by ejaculation. This assumption may not be correct.

Reinforcement of Fear

As with most of the other hypotheses, the drive-reduction one has difficulty with the relationship between pain and fear. Common sense says that it is the onset of pain that reinforces the fear, but according to the drive-reduction hypothesis, it must be the offset. Experiments in which the offset of pain is delayed, do not produce the less efficient learning of fear to be expected from the gradient of reinforcement (Mowrer and Solomon, 1954; Fromer, 1962). There are a number of ways of explaining this, each of which could be tested by an experiment that would have some general value quite outside of this particular controversy. But these results clearly place the burden of proof on supporters of the drive-reduction hypothesis, so that their position is weakened until their alibis are experimentally verified. Let me briefly describe the rationale of some experiments.

In most situations used to investigate the gradient of rein-forcement, the response at the moment of reinforcement is different from the one for which the reinforcement has been delayed. When the response is relatively similar throughout the interval of delay, as in running from the start toward the goal of a straight alley, the gradient of reinforcement is reasonably flat, as Judson Brown (1948) has shown with the strength-of-pull tech-nique. Yet other experiments show that variability of responses during the delay interval increases the steepness of the gradient (Kimble, 1961). Now if one thinks of fear as the component of the pain response that can be attached to new cues by learning, then it follows that fear must persist as a constant response throughout the pain. Perhaps this is why it is reinforced by pain while other responses preceding the onset of pain and usually interrupted by incompatible responses during the pain, are not.

Whenever a response persists in unchanged form, perhaps the interval that should be measured is not the one between the conditioned onset of the response and reinforcement, but the interval between the termination of (or change in) the response and reinforcement. If so, the response of fear to pain would always be reinforced by immediate association with the end of pain. In any event, an answer to the problem of which interval is the relevant one should have general significance.

One test would be to train rats to start licking at a drink-ometer tube as soon as a light starts to flash. They should be shaped until they will lick for the same ten seconds used in the fear experiment before receiving water. Then the test should be to condition the licking to another stimulus, such as a tone, under two conditions: (1) either when the water is delivered practically immediately, or (2) when the water is delivered at the end of ten seconds of licking. Under these circumstances, will the ten seconds of delay produce a measurable decrement?

Another different possibility is that the biggest burst of pain occurs immediately after the onset of shock and is followed by a relatively rapid adaptation down to a lower level, so that the majority of drive reduction always occurs shortly after onset. In principle, this hypothesis can be tested by central recording, ideally with microelectrodes in a variety of points along the central pathways in the brain, and up to the highest sensory projections of pain. Perhaps my colleagues here will tell me that this already has been done. Such work ought to have some interest in its own right, in addition to its relevance to the pain-fear paradox in reinforcement.

Unfortunate Indeterminancy

The evidence that animals will learn responses to explore or to manipulate has been used as an argument against the drive-reduction hypothesis, but the force of this argument is weakened somewhat by the fact that, where it has been carefully investigated, such activity has been found to show satiation (Harlow, 1950; Butler, 1957). If one wants to think in terms of a general drive, such as boredom, it would be important to show that being presented with a great variety of fascinating opportunities to explore would produce at least some transient general satiation that would show up on exploring something new. If the satiation is highly specific, it would be more plausible to assume that the reinforcement is based on the arousal response of the reticular formation which shows habituation that is limited to each specific type of new stimulation that is introduced and then repeated.

As I have pointed out before (Miller, 1959) in situations in which strong sources of stimulation under external control (such as very bright lights, intense sounds, strong electric shocks, etc.) are suddenly turned off, one can be reasonably certain that there is a reduction in stimulus intensity and the results also show that learning and performance vary with the intensity of the drive, which in turn is directly related to the amount of drive reduction. In situations where there is no independent measure of the drive, it is difficult to say whether or not drive reduction has occurred. Unfortunately, many situations are of the latter kind, so that it is difficult to prove that the drive-reduction hypothesis is wrong, but at present one can make the more damning statement that it is irrelevant.

Central Stimulation and Recording[5]

The foregoing difficulty with the drive reduction hypothesis is one of the reasons why I started probing around inside of the brain. I hope that if one can locate centers which when stimulated show all of the functional properties of a given drive, one may be able to use recording from such "centers" as measures of the drive.

I also think that by manipulating drives in very unusual ways, one may be able to test for the direction of the casual relation involved in the correlation between drive-reduction (i.e., satiation) and reward. In short, evolution would be almost certain to select animals that are rewarded by events satiating their drives, but this does not necessarily mean that the drive-reduction produces the reward. If the correlation is indeed spurious, it should be more likely to disappear when drives are manipulated in unnatural ways that have not been involved in the survival of the fittest.

Recent results are beginning to make it look as though the correlation may indeed be spurious. Thus, Robinson and Mishkin (1962) have investigated a number of different points in the monkey's brain from which electrical stimulation elicits eating. If this stimulation elicits hunger, the drive-reduction hypothesis demands that its offset be rewarding. At some of these points the monkeys will work to turn off the stimulation, at others they will work to turn it on, and at still others the stimulation seems to be completely neutral. Unfortunately, they have not investi-

---

[5] See also Miller (1960, 1961c): 1961c, for a discussion of the implications of rewarding effects of central stimulation.

gated these points to see whether the effects of stimulation there have the other functional properties of normal hunger, so that it is conceivable that the stimulation is merely eliciting gnawing reflexes. But it seems only fair to put the burden of proof for such a possibility on the supporters of the drive-reduction hypothesis.

OPTIMAL-LEVEL HYPOTHESIS

Another hypothesis is that each type of stimulation has an optimum level, with any shift away from the optimum being motivating, and any shift toward it being rewarding. This hypothesis is superficially attractive and may well be true. The hedonic hypothesis is a special case of this one in which the optimal level for aversive stimuli is zero and for satisfying ones is as high as possible. But this hypothesis allows for the possibility of other stimuli for which the optimal level is somewhere in between.

The extra flexibility of this hypothesis, however, is produced at a price. Not only must we have a catalog of all the stimuli, but also of their optimal levels, and of how important deviations are from these levels. There is little economy over the empirical law of effect and the same difficulty with the pain-fear paradox. If some independent means of determining optimal level could be devised, it would materially change the status of this hypothesis.

CENTRAL CONFIRMING RESPONSE

Thorndike (1933) originally put forward the idea that there might be some kind of a central confirming response which strengthened any learnable connections that had been active just before it occurred. It is easier to imagine that some single mechanism has been evolved for this purpose than that each of the many diverse rewards exerts its effect independently. Such a mechanism would have the parsimonious economy of the drive-reduction hypothesis without many of its limitations.

This general idea is worth reviving now, because technical advances may make it possible to investigate directly such an activity of the nervous system. If only one such mechanism is involved, however, we run into our old friend, the pain-fear

paradox—why does the onset of pain not reinforce other responses
in addition to fear? Let us hope that this can be clarified by some
of the experiments I have suggested. As I shall show, we may be
able to escape it by a notion similar to, yet crucially different
from, the confirming response.

Puzzling Deficit from Hippocampal Lesions

Clinical observations and a certain number of experimental
studies of patients with bilateral lesions in the hippocampal area
(Milner, 1959; 1962) pose difficulties for most other hypotheses
and increase the attractiveness of the confirming response. Such
patients do not have marked deficits in immediate memory, so
that they can carry on a conversation more or less normally.
They also do not have obvious deficits in memory for events that
occurred long enough before the lesion, so that apparently the
mechanism for storing such memories is not impaired. They do
have a marked deficit, however, in their ability to acquire new
long-term memories, so that, for example, they fail to show any
improvement at a variety of simple learning tasks, with the
interesting exception of mirror drawing (Milner, 1962).

It is conceivable that such a deficit could be explained in
terms of a failure of the mechanisms for pleasure-pain, drive-
reduction, or optimal level, but in that case one would think
that the failure of reinforcement would produce experimental
extinction as well as failure to learn. It is somewhat easier to
think of this intriguing deficit as a failure of a confirmatory
response, but one might be forced to the position of concluding
that this response was necessary for learning but not to prevent
experimental extinction. Do such subjects show experimental
extinction of previously learned habits? If not, we may have
evidence supporting the notion that extinction and new learning
are basically similar. Obviously, these fascinating cases need to be
further investigated so that the exact nature of the defect can be
precisely delimited.

Role of DC Potentials

One conceivable candidate for a "confirming response" is
the DC potential that Rusinov (1953), Morrell (1961), and others

have found can be used to establish a temporary connection. Thus far the technique has been to apply a positive potential to a small part of the surface of the motor cortex first, after which a previously ineffective stimulus will elicit a response specific to that part of the cortex. After a number of such elicitations, the response continues even after the DC potential is withdrawn, but becomes progressively weaker as if it were showing experimental extinction.

Of course, the resemblance to learning may turn out to be only superficial, or the DC potential may be a highly abnormal way of producing a change which is indeed involved in typical learning, but normally is produced by some quite different means. Nevertheless, it is interesting that Rowland (1963) has observed changes in DC potentials during learning. Furthermore, Morrell (1963), in an article presenting many other fascinating and challenging results, gives evidence indicating that a negative potential on the cortex, at a low level which does not produce other obvious effects, will interfere with learning.

Certain further questions should be investigated. Will the DC potential serve as a reinforcement if it is applied briefly immediately after a response or, in other words, in the same sequence that is effective for normal reward? Let us say that food reward is used to train an animal to lift its paw when a mild vibratory stimulus is applied to it. Could brief DC potentials be substituted for the food in maintaining this response? Could they be used to establish some new CR? If positive results should be secured in such an experiment, it would be interesting to find out whether DC potential would have similar rewarding effects in other parts of the brain where the cells are not lined up in the same regular way.

Finally, I come to a speculation which I would only dare put forward in the presence of colleagues who have the knowledge to correct me if it is completely ridiculous, and the tact to do so kindly. Is it possible that lesions in the hippocampal cortex remove active tissue normally generating negative potentials down there and hence disturb volume conduction of the brain in such a way that it is harder for a sufficient positive potential to be generated on the surface of the nearby overlying speech and association areas? Could such patients be improved by supplying a suitable weak positive bias there, or a negative bias where the lesion was made?

If these particular speculations are fantastic, some shrewder ones coupled with greater technical skill may solve the problem of locating a confirmatory reaction.

GUTHRIE'S CONTIGUITY HYPOTHESIS

With characteristic ingenuity, Guthrie (1952) has proposed that the function of reward is not to strengthen previously formed connections which are presumed to be established solely by contiguity, but to produce a stimulus change which protects them from being unlearned by retroactive inhibition. This proposal has attractive simplicity: it is easy to imagine how such a mechanism might work. But if it is sheer stimulus change that is effective, one might think that responses leading to electric shock would be protected by that drastic change from being unlearned. One of Guthrie's outs on this is that the shock elicits withdrawal responses that are incompatible with approach. We have already discussed this aspect of the pain-fear paradox and how it might further be investigated.

Another possibility is to say that it is only the removal of stimulus elements that preserves responses to them from being subject to retroactive inhibition. In that case one wonders why a person who is turning around so that the last thing that he does to the sight of the front-wall is to turn to the left, and the last thing he does to the side-wall is to turn left, and so on, until he is facing the front-wall again, does not continue spinning indefinitely. Guthrie dodges this difficulty by suggesting that the most effective changes are the removal of the maintaining stimuli, namely the ones that are responsible for the action. This comes close to the drive-reduction hypothesis although, of course, the underlying mechanism, protection, rather than strengthening, is different. If one says that protection is more effective the greater the number of stimulus elements that are removed, the hypothesis becomes more similar to the strong-stimulus reduction one.

In any event, it would seem desirable to try to train an

animal in a discrimination until a response was highly specific to a CS which was withdrawn as soon as this response was performed. In terms of Guthrie's hypothesis, it is hard to see how such a response would become extinguished; instead, each time it was repeated it should become attached to any aberrant members of the population of cues elicited by the CS that had previously failed to occur and hence had not yet become conditioners for it. Perhaps this will happen.

Similarly, it is hard to see how Guthrie could explain the fact that with prolonged practice a delayed conditioned response to a cue that persists for a number of seconds tends to move back nearer to the point of reinforcement. Finally, it is hard to see how Guthrie can explain the increase in vigor which frequently occurs during a series of reinforced trials.

Consummatory Response Hypothesis

Sheffield, Roby, and Campbell (1954) have proposed a drive-induction hypothesis. According to this hypothesis, the consummatory response tends to be conditioned to responses immediately preceding it, but since it cannot occur in the absence of the goal object, frustrational excitement is elicited which serves as an increase in drive that energizes whatever response is occurring at that time. The cues involved in responses leading most directly to the consummatory responses are conditioned most strongly to it. Hence, when the subject is oscillating at a choice point, the responses leading most directly to the goal produce the most exciting cues, are more invigorated by this excitement, and are most likely to be continued. Such responses are also conditioned by contiguity and hence are more likely than others to be elicited immediately on subsequent trials. It can be seen that this hypothesis accounts for the increase in vigor which is difficult for Guthrie.

One of the main difficulties with this hypothesis is that it places too much emphasis on the peripheral consummatory response. For example, an animal's consumption of a new food is not necessarily avid immediately after the feedback from the initial bite, but increases gradually with experience. How is this increase in the consummatory response learned? The problem is still more pointed in an experiment like the one performed by Harris, et al. (1933) in which animals deficient in Vitamin B apparently did not have any immediate preference for a solution containing a minute amount of the purified extract, but could learn to prefer such a solution, provided it was given a distinctive flavor. That this consummatory response was not controlled by immediate feedback from the taste of the vitamin was shown by the fact that, when the vitamin was put in a different solution, they only gradually learned to abandon the original one and go to the new one. It is difficult to account for such learning on the assumption that the vigor of performance of the peripheral consummatory response is the crucial factor in determining reinforcement. Observations by Weiskrantz and Cowey (1963) present a similar difficulty. Such results suggest that reinforcement is the crucial factor in determining the vigor of the consummatory response.

Furthermore, Marion Kessen and I (1952) have shown that rats will learn to go to the side of a T-maze where milk is delivered directly into their stomachs, thereby completely by-passing the consummatory response. It is barely possible that the slight amount of reflex licking sometimes observed while milk is being given via fistula could be considered enough of a consummatory response to mediate such learning. But this way out is not very adequate because such licking occurs in the absence of the goal object, and hence presumably could become anticipatory without being blocked by absence of a goal object. Therefore, Sheffield's frustrational mechanism for inducing excitement does not seem to be present.

It would be still more difficult to account for learning reinforced by injecting sugar or water directly into the bloodstream of a hungry or thirsty animal. But I do not like the techniques that Coppock and Chambers (1954) have used to get presumably positive results on this problem, because they involve measuring the total time spent on one of two sides of an apparatus in which the injection is given. To give an extreme example, if subjects continue to explore randomly, but are completely knocked out every time they go to the injection side, it is obvious that they will spend more time there, without necessarily having learned to go there. That is why techniques for measuring frequency of choice are better. A recent experiment by Clark, et al. (1961) indicates that a thirsty monkey will learn to press a bar to get isotonic saline injected into his bloodstream, but will not press when he is satiated on water. We need more experiments of this kind.

Finally, in an addendum to a mimeographed paper for which he should not be held too accountable because it is unpublished, Sheffield (1954) deals with the problem of learning to escape and avoid painful shocks by assuming that the conditioned induction of the drive of fear functions as excitement. Therefore, it would lead to approach to an electric shock if it were not for the incompatible responses elicited by the shock. With admirable clarity he says: "Any punishment situation which could be rigged to prevent the moving forward of an incompatible terminal response would be expected to produce the paradoxical strengthening of the response that leads to punishment." Perhaps this will indeed be true in the choice experiment which I have proposed with shock to the hind-feet. We shall see.

Incidentally, any hypothesis that attributes generalized reinforcing value to *the elicitation of a prepotent response* may have trouble by predicting that the subject will learn the response leading to an electric shock which elicits a prepotent wild leap. The same difficulty applies to Premack (1959) who concludes that whenever a strong response, emitted at a higher rate, is made contingent upon the prior occurrence of a weaker response, emitted at a lower rate, the latter is reinforced by the former. A rat's rate of running in an activity wheel can be greatly increased by avoidance training in which every time that he stops he receives a shock that can be turned off only by running. But I do not believe that such an increase in the rate of wheel turning would increase the rate at which rats would press a bar to unlock the wheel and turn on the shock which would produce the fast rate. Nevertheless, the experiment should be tried.

TOLMAN'S EXPECTANCY HYPOTHESIS

According to Tolman (1932), the animal learns "what leads to what" by the contiguous association of various experiences. Thus he may learn that a specific alley leads to food by exploring a maze when not hungry. The law of effect is not required for such learning. Then when hungry, he displays this latent learning by going down that alley to food. Similarly, in classical conditioning, the animal learns to associate the sound of the bell with the delivery and taste of food, and hence on a test trial salivates because he expects the food after the bell. As has often been pointed out, such a theory is weak on specifying just how the expectation leads to appropriate action.

Various attempts to correct this weakness have still left the skeptics feeling that most of the predictive power of the theory does not follow rigorously from the assumptions, but rather from having the reader think of what he would do in that situation, thereby using his experience with observing his own behavior as a basis for predicting the subject's behavior. Essentially, this procedure reduces to saying that one organism will behave like another one; it is an actuarial type of prediction. Perhaps the technique of computer simulation can now be used to test whether Tolman's assumptions actually will lead to the predicted behavior without the help of the reader's intuition.

The strength of such a theory is that it does predict the latent learning and the sensory preconditioning which sometimes can be observed. Its weakness is that, when applied to lower animals, it predicts much more sensory preconditioning and latent learning than actually occurs.

A Rigorous Test of Latent Learning

To cite one experiment, DeBold and I (Miller, 1961d) paired a flashing light with an injection of water into a rat's mouth via a fistula. During this training, one group of animals was super-satiated on water, having been given more than they normally would have drunk, another group was normally satiated, a third group was moderately thirsty and a fourth was quite thirsty. When subsequently tested under thirst, the animals trained under moderate drive showed a moderate amount of conditioned tongue licking, those trained under strong drive showed a great deal more, and the first two groups were indistinguishable from controls. If conditioning is primarily a matter of learning "what leads to what" by sheer contiguity, it is hard to understand how the satiated rats could have escaped learning that the light was going to be followed by an injection of water into their mouths. If the tongue licking of the animals with appropriate drive is explained on the basis of such an expectation, it is hard to see why the satiated animals who were subsequently made thirsty showed no such learning.

Nevertheless, it should be noted that, as one moves up the scale from lower vertebrates to man, the total picture of behavior does become more like that depicted in Tolman's theory although there still are a number of exceptions. Finally, I should point out that Tolman's approach does not encounter difficulty with the pain-fear paradox.

In short, while S-R theories do well in predicting stupid behavior, but are much less convincing in predicting intelligent behavior, Tolman seems to do well in dealing with intelligence, but has trouble in dealing with stupidity. Is there some way to deal adequately with both?

Mowrer's Motivational Feedback Hypothesis

Mowrer's (1960a) latest hypothesis is that only motivational responses are acquired during learning, and that these are acquired by classical conditioning involving only contiguity. A response is guided by the emotional feedback conditioned to the cues that it produces, much as the excitement initially favors certain responses in Sheffield's hypothesis. Thus, if a response produces cues to which fear has been conditioned, it tends to be abandoned. If a response produces cues to which hope has been conditioned, it tends to be continued. Such feedback guides the responses much in the same way that a blindfolded person's movements may be guided in a parlor game by saying, "You're getting hotter," or, "You're getting colder." According to his theory, the law of effect does *not* directly strengthen any motor responses to cues; it only serves to steer such motor responses so that they home in on a beam of hope.

This hypothesis avoids the pain-fear paradox by abandoning the idea that motor responses to cues are strengthened by reinforcement; it also predicts the kind of flexibility which is observed as such a prominent feature of most behavior. However, it is hard to see how it ever could predict the rapid selection of one out of a great number of different alternative responses, each of which would have to be tentatively sampled and continued or discontinued on the basis of the emotions conditioned to its sensory feedback. On this basis, how could a speaker ever select in time the correct one out of the thirty thousand commonest words in his vocabulary, or how could a skilled typist select the finger movements that would hit the right keys in rapid succession? Mowrer (1960a) seems to recognize this difficulty and says he will solve it in his second book (1960b), but he does not. It remains as a fatal weakness.

How the Miller-Dollard Cybernetic Hypothesis Accounts for Learning Rapid Performance

Mowrer's (1960a) theory will be recognized as similar in many respects to the analysis of copying which Dollard and I (Miller and Dollard, 1941) published a little over twenty years ago, and which I have since been extending to other types of behavior such as goal-directed learned drives and the approximation of centrally represented standards (Miller, 1951; 1959, pp. 248–250; 1963b). Mowrer has made a contribution in spelling out in more detail how behavior can be shaped by learned drive-induction, and learned drive-reduction, but in my opinion has snared himself in insuperable difficulties by abandoning the notion of any learned connection between stimuli and motor responses. By retaining such connections, but extending the notion of cue to include a discrepancy and extending the notion of response to include a motor change in a given direction, our analysis shows how cybernetically guided behavior can become faster with practice in the following "stages":

1. In the initial stages of dealing with an unfamiliar situation, behavior may be guided solely by the drive-inducing and drive-reducing "responses" attached to various cues. Then it should be quite slow and erratic, something like the very first trial at mirror drawing because there are no correct directional responses attached to directional cues.

2.   Ordinarily, at the same time that the subject is learning to attach secondary reinforcing responses to certain cues and drive-inducing ones to others, he will be expected to be learning to respond to the cue of the direction of a difference with a directional response that will tend to reduce the difference. Such responses should reduce wildly erratic responses and give behavior a goal-directed quality. It should be understood that one correction tends to blend into another, so that when I speak of a cue and a response, I am talking of a cross section of a dynamic process which is continuous at a molar level, but may or may not consist of discrete quantal "units" at a micro level.

3.   With further practice, the subject should begin to learn to respond also to the magnitude of the difference by responding to larger differences with larger correctional responses, and to smaller differences with smaller corrections. As he learns to make more accurate initial corrections, he will need less guidance by subsequent feedback, so that his response can be greatly speeded up. Eventually, his initial response may become accurate enough so that it will need no subsequent correction. Then the response will be more ballistic than cybernetic.

Obviously, the foregoing stages are not distinct, but blend into one another. Another complication is that one form of feedback may be progressively substituted for another. For example, in a rotary pursuit task, proprioceptive feedback may be substituted for visual feedback, and where predictable sequences must be run off very rapidly, it is possible that central feedback may be substituted for peripheral feedback.[6]

I believe that the roles of the different types of responses postulated in the first stages of the sequence can be demonstrated in a psychomotor task by changing the input-output effect of the control lever. Thus, a reversal of direction should be disruptive from practically the very beginning, except for a subject who had learned to adjust appropriately to such a reversal. But drastic fluctuations in the magnitude of the correction required to the cue of a specific discrepancy should not be as disruptive in

[6] For a further discussion of responses see Miller (1959, pp. 238–52).

the very earliest stages before the subject had learned to respond with an appropriate magnitude of correction.

Finally, I believe that responses can be greatly speeded up by being tied together into larger functional units. Thus, the typist for whom a word is a unit can go much faster than the one for whom the single letter is the unit and, I predict, would be less likely to be stopped in the middle of a word if the feedback were radically changed by suddenly freezing the keys.[7] But without something like stimulus-response connections, I find it difficult to see how responses can be assembled together into larger functional units.

At the same time I agree that these larger units are controlled by their feedback, so that something like the heirarchy of "plans" described by Miller, Galanter, and Pribram (1960) can play a very important role, which needs to be worked out and investigated in more detail. In fact, I believe that the feedback signalling that a discrepancy has been removed and a subgoal achieved almost certainly acts as a reinforcement. In terms of the analysis subsequently advanced by Miller, Galanter, and Pribram, the steps that I have listed above might be thought of as ways in which the operate phase of a TOTE sequence becomes more efficient as a result of experience involving reinforcement by achieving the subgoal (i.e., exit) of removing the discrepancy. It is my opinion that plans, hierarchies of plans, or programs for processing information are affected by rewards in the same way as simpler "responses."

Two-Factor Hypothesis

One popular way out of the pain-fear paradox is to assume that there are two different mechanisms of reinforcement, the law of effect for certain types of learning and classical conditioning by contiguity alone for others. But if one has two different mechanisms of reinforcement, one wants to know when to apply

---

[7] This might be a way of accurately measuring the role of peripheral feedback (how many milliseconds and how many letters before the first disturbance was noted in performance? What are the effects of interfering with feedback at the beginning or the end of a unit such as a word?)

which mechanism to what. It is somewhat circular simply to apply whichever mechanism fits.

Are Visceral Responses Subject to the Law of Effect?

The most frequent solution to this problem has been to assume that glandular and visceral responses under the control of the autonomic nervous system are subject only to classical conditioning with contiguity being sufficient, while responses of the skeletal muscalature under the control of the somatic nervous system are subject to the law of effect (cf. Skinner, 1938; Mowrer, 1947; Solomon & Wynne, 1954). In addition to resolving the pain-fear paradox, this hypothesis seems to fit the experimental facts, although there is a certain amount of debate about whether skeletal muscle responses are subject to genuine classical conditioning in addition to the law of effect (Kimble, 1961). Furthermore, such a distinction fits in with the dramatic peripheral difference between the autonomic and the spinal nervous system, and with the historical tradition of considering the former to involve a lower, vegetative order of functioning (MacLean, 1960).

On the other hand, as one goes up into the brain where learned connections presumably are formed, these two systems become intimately intermingled. Furthermore, it seems plausible that we do not observe visceral responses being modified by the law of effect because they are internal responses which ordinarily do not affect the external environment and hence cannot be instrumental in securing reward in the everyday life of the animal. Perhaps they do not show this kind of learning because they ordinarily are not subject to this kind of training (Miller, 1961b).

It should be noted that most human subjects have not been rewarded for contracting the skeletal muscles that move the ears and do not have voluntary control of such movements, while a visceral response which does have an effect on the external environment, namely that of the urethral sphincter, does seem to be modified by a course of social training involving rewards and punishment; it is brought under voluntary control which is indistinguishable from that exerted over the majority of skeletal muscles. Furthermore, there is a considerable array of evidence that under special circumstances other visceral responses can be made to behave as though they were governed by the law of effect (e.g., Barber, 1961).

From the point of view of learning theory, it is important to determine as unequivocally as possible, whether or not mammalian learning is governed by two different mechanisms of reinforcement, applying respectively to the somatic and visceral systems. Whichever way this question is answered will narrow down the range of alternatives to be considered by theorists and hence will be an important step toward converging on a basic understanding of the process of learning.

The same problem also is important for psychosomatic medicine. If visceral responses can be modified only by classical conditioning, then a given visceral response can be reinforced only by the limited number of stimuli which produce the same kind of a response. But if such responses are subject to the law of effect, their learning can be reinforced by any one of a large number of rewards, irrespective of whether or not these produce that kind of unconditioned visceral response. Furthermore, the motivation and reward of such responses can be transferred from one type of motivation to another, just as a rat which has learned to press a bar to get food when hungry can readily be taught to continue pressing to get water when thirsty.

For example, if visceral responses can be reinforced by the law of effect, a child who is terrified by an examination for which he feels unprepared and happens to develop a stomach upset which then leads to his being excused from school might be reinforced by escape from fear and acquire a tendency to respond to similar situations with stomach symptoms. Another child who has a fainting spell might learn to become more susceptible to fainting. If such responses are acquired, they might be reinforced by yet other secondary gains. But we have no firm experimental evidence that this can in fact occur.

The most direct approach to the problem is to try to use suitable instrumentation to record a visceral response, such as a change in heart rate and then try to reward this in exactly the same way as one would a skeletal response. Shearn (1961) has secured evidence showing that the human heart rate can indeed be modified in this way. These results can be interpreted as showing only that the subjects have learned some response of the skeletal muscles which in turn has an automatic effect on heart rate. In order to rule this out, we are starting to work on dogs under curare which blocks responses of the skeletal muscles and requires artificial respiration. Solomon and Turner (1962) have evidence that the heart rate can be modified by classical conditioning under such conditions.

Danger of False Negative Results

We have mentioned the necessity, which long has been recognized, of ruling out changes produced by indirect means which might produce false positive results. But there is also a danger of securing false negative results, which may account for the failures of such informal experiments as have been mentioned in the literature (Skinner, 1938; Mowrer, 1938). As Hebb (1949) has trenchantly pointed out, most of the learning studied in the laboratory involves an enormous amount of transfer of training. The rat, which learns to use its paw to press a bar, already has had a great deal of practice in using his paws for other purposes. When we start without the benefit of such transfer of training, we may find that initial learning is much slower and more difficult than we had imagined. You may get some idea of this if you try to learn to wiggle one of your ears independently, a response of the skeletal muscles for which adequate innervation is available, and which has been learned by at least one individual whom I have personally observed. But in the long run, this difficulty could turn out to be an advantage because it could give us an opportunity to observe the early phases of learning that is not aided by massive transfer of training.

Central vs. Peripheral Responses

Deutsch (1956) and Broadbent (1961) have proposed a somewhat different two-factor theory involving contiguity for the central responses involved in imagery, and reward for overt motor responses. It is hard for me to imagine a basis for such a dichotomy unless, as I have suggested, the central responses require less reward for their maintenance because they require less effort (Miller, 1959, p. 246). But this would not be a genuine dichotomy. Conceivably, the particular line-up of the cells in the motor cortex could make them more susceptible to DC potentials, or to some other factor involved in the action of reward. But the intimate relationship between speech and thinking appears to argue against a basic dichotomy between the mechanisms for the reinforcement of overt and central responses.

Deutsch (1956) feels that without his dichotomy, a child who went to a given room in the expectation of receiving an ice-cream cone would have this expectation rewarded if he were given money there. Then, according to Deutsch, the child should continue to go to that room whenever hungry.

My opinion is that, if the child were given the money *before* he reached an ice-cream vending machine which he never went on to inspect, and if the receipt of the money could be made dependent upon having the image of an ice-cream cone, he would continue to have such an image. But I must report that my one very brief experimental attempt to use food as a reward to reinforce a conditioned action potential in the visual cortex of a cat did not immediately lead to spectacular success (Miller, 1961d). Such a problem is, however, open to further investigation by experimental means.

Finally, I believe that, if a child had the opportunity to see that the ice-cream cone machine was empty, the perception of the empty machine would override the image of the ice-cream cone, so that any money given afterward would reinforce the image of no ice cream more strongly than that of ice cream. I suspect that this is the way to escape from Deutsch's dilemma.

I believe that the human tendency to indulge in wishful thinking, rationalization, and repression, as well as human susceptibility to certain types of persuasion, indicate that the central responses involved in thinking are affected by reward. Children have no separate mechanism that automatically avoids wishful thinking, they have to learn by rewards and punishments to be realistic.

Motivational Effects of All Good UCS

If one makes a list of the most effective unconditioned stimuli for classical conditioning, one is struck by the fact that either the onset or offset of so many of these can serve as a reward for trial and error behavior. This tends to suggest a one-factor theory. But are there any exceptions? Most of the supposed exceptions that I can think of are borderline cases. Thus, there is some question whether or not the pupillary dilation to reduction in illumination can be conditioned when other factors, such as the point of fixation, are adequately controlled. There is also some evidence suggesting that similar changes in illumination may have a weak reinforcing effect on an instrumental response, such as pressing a bar.

It would be worthwhile to investigate other apparent exceptions more carefully.

For example, Bykov's (1957) work indicates that the inhibition of the antidiuretic hormones can be conditioned. Would an animal that was overloaded with water learn to press a bar to turn off an intravenous infusion of antidiuretic hormone administered via a chronic catheter?

Phylogenetic Sequence of Learning?

The two-factor hypothesis suggests a careful examination of lower vertebrates which seem to be on as direct as possible a line of evolution toward the mammalian nervous system. Does trial-and-error learning rewarded by the law of effect emerge earlier, later, or at the same time as classical conditioning apparently reinforced by contiguity? Such investigations will have to be sophisticated, however, in order not to be mislead by various artifacts such as "sensitization" and also must involve a good enough knowledge of the animal's behavior repertoire to allow the experimenter to provide an equal opportunity for both kinds of learning to occur.

We also need highly sophisticated investigations of the degree to which both types of learning are removed when higher parts of the brain are removed, but the experimenter must set up conditions under which it is possible for one of two responses to be differentially reinforced by reward or by escape from punishment. We should also bear in mind here the possibility of securing false negative results if we use responses that are not aided by the normal amount of transfer of training.

My Alternative to Drive Reduction

In one scene of a motion picture (Miller and Hart, 1948), an experimentally naïve rat has been scrambling around on an electrified grid for a while without securing more than momentary relief. Finally, he happens to rotate a wheel which turns off the shock. This initial response is not vigorous. But immediately afterward, almost like an actor doing a "second take," he starts to rotate the wheel furiously.

My interpretation of such observations has been that the sudden reduction in pain strengthened the connection from pain, fear, and all of the other functioning cues in the situation, to the response of rotating the wheel. In other words, I assumed that the reinforcement produced by drive reduction caused the increase in vigor of this response. This may be true. But what happens if one assumes that the causal relationship runs in the opposite direction?

Let us explore the assumption that the sudden relief from pain produces an automatic increase in the activity of any neural circuits that have just been firing. Let us further assume that it is this energization that is responsible for the strong performance (in this case appearing as vigorous overt rehearsal) which in turn is responsible for learning by contiguity. Such energization could involve the reticular activating system or it could involve something as different as a DC potential. Let us see where such speculations can lead us.

There are a number of ways of proceeding from this point. At one extreme, one can assume that each of the stimulus situations in the long list known to be empirically rewarding is individually wired up so that it will have its own separate network (DC potential or other means) for facilitating any ongoing activity, including the trace of an immediately preceding activity. At the other extreme, one can assume that there is a single "go network" or "go mechanism." It is obvious that the latter would be much more parsimonious to construct, but natural selection does not always result in maximum parsimony.

Let us make the following tentative assumptions:

1. *That there are one or more "go" or "activating" mechanisms in the brain which act to intensify ongoing responses to cues and the traces of immediately preceding activities, producing a stronger intensification the more strongly the "go mechanism" is activated.*

2. *That this "go mechanism" (or "mechanisms," as will be understood but not repeated hereafter) can be activated in a variety of ways, such as by reduction in noxious stimulation, by the taste of food to a hungry animal, possibly by feedback from still more central effects of eating, by the release of a stimulated but inhibited response from blocking, by the removal of a discrepancy between an intention and an achievement, etc.* The similarity between the "go" mechanism and the "confirming response" will be recognized, but it is assumed that the primary effect of the "go" mechanism is to intensify current activities, including dynamic or other traces, rather than *directly* to strengthen connections. As will be seen from *3* and *4* below, however, a secondary effect of such intensification is to strengthen corrections, or in other words, habits.

3. *That all responses, including the activation of this "go mechanism" are subject to conditioning with contiguity being sufficient.* Note that this is a crucial difference from Mowrer (1960a and 1960b) which avoids the fatal weakness that has already been pointed out.

4. *That the strength of the CR is determined to a great degree by the strength of the UCR (including the intensified trace which automatically serves as a UCR since the activities are similar), but also by the number of pairings.* This is a key assumption, which together with the preceding ones, means that more strongly rewarded responses will be prepotent over competing less strongly rewarded ones. The number of pairings could act to build up more functional units in an all-or-none way as Guthrie (1952) assumes; we do not need to decide that point now.

5. *That when a chain of cues leads to a UCS for the "go mechanism", it is most strongly conditioned to those nearer to*

the UCS, but can be conditioned (perhaps via lingering traces and/or by successive higher-order conditioning) to those farther away with a progressive decline in strength.

6. *That every time a CR (including a conditioned "go response") is repeated without reinforcement from the UCS (or perhaps it should be, a CS is presented without a UCS, or the CR is stronger than the UCR), it is subject to a certain amount of weakening, or in other words, experimental extinction.* With instrumental responses it will be remembered that the intensified trace serves as the UCS, so that non-intensification of the trace will, according to the present assumption, produce experimental extinction.

It can be seen that, after various conditioning trials in its environment, an organism or other device, constructed along these principles, would tend to be guided cybernetically toward the UCS for the "go system," and that it would tend to drop out sequences that doubled back on themselves (blind alleys). It also would learn specific S-R connections[8] which could be the basis for immediate choice, without the necessity for sampling various cues, or in other words, showing VTE's before every choice. Thus the theory avoids the fatal weakness of Mowrer's (1960a and 1960b) formulation. Such an organism would learn fear by classical conditioning, but would not learn to approach pain, because it is only the offset of pain that is the UCS for the "go" mechanism.

In developing this line of speculation I use the extended definitions of stimulus and response, including central activities and attention, which were advanced before such notions were fashionable (Miller and Dollard, 1941), and have been repeated and extended recently (Miller, 1959, pp. 238–252; 1963b), includ-

---

[8] Please note carefully that the word "connection" is used in the sense defined by Miller and Dollard (1941 p. 21): "The word 'connection' is used to refer to a causal sequence, the details of which are practically unknown, rather than to specific neural strands." There is nothing to prevent a "connection" from being a modulation of an ongoing activity, a complex processing of information, or a complex pattern of permanent traces in different parts of different networks, provided that the end result is that under specified conditions a cue has a tendency to be followed by a response, as we have broadly defined both of these terms.

ing the extension to different "programs" suggested in this paper. The key assumption is that all of these apparently diverse processes follow the same basic laws of learning (Miller, 1959, p. 243).

Some Similarities and Differences with Other Theories

The present hypothesis has obvious resemblances to Mowrer (1960a, 1960b) except for the crucial fact that, like the original analysis of copying (Miller and Dollard, 1941), it does *not* rule out connections between cues and motor responses, and therefore does have a way of eliciting immediate responses. Thus, it overcomes a fatal weakness of Mowrer's theory.

The present formulation also resembles Sheffield's (1954) drive-induction hypothesis, and some of the recent emphasis by Spence (1956) on the incentive value of the anticipatory goal response, except that it does *not* limit itself to incentives based on the conditioning of peripheral consummatory responses, and does specifically include an incentive based on the termination of noxious stimulation.[9] While Spence, who has primarily used the empirical law of effect, prudently has not clearly made up his mind, the present formulation differs from what seems to be Spence's present position in that it clearly and definitely does not assume different processes for appetitive and aversive learning, or for the acquisition of habit strength and incentive strength.

While the present formulation does use association by contiguity, it differs from Guthrie (1952) in using the booster or "go mechanism" to explain the obvious selectivity of learning, instead of relying on stimulus change to protect certain elements of completely indiscriminate learning from being unlearned. It also differs from Guthrie in having a specific assumption about

[9] In his latest version of his drive-induction hypothesis, Sheffield (1960) is moving toward a "central response" position, more similar to the one advanced in the present paper, but he still seems to emphasize the consummatory response. In discussing the problem of what aspect of the consummatory response is conditionable and what aspect moves forward to produce consummatory excitement, he says: "...we will all have to give up the idea that what moves forward is some overt or peripheral portion of the consummatory response. I am already thinking instead of a central-nervous-system phenomenon which may show up in various ways at the behavioral level."

experimental extinction. Conceivably, this assumption can later be derived from the more basic phenomenon of habituation, or from the learning of interfering activities, but this is a tricky problem.

The present formulation is similar to Tolman (1932) in that reward serves to elicit performance and that there is a possibility of learning by contiguity. It differs, however, in (a) that activated performance clearly is essential for the learning of responses, including central ones, that must compete with other strong responses at the time of such learning or that are strong enough to do so during performance, and (b) that it is assumed that direct responses can be learned without always having an expectancy as a mediating link. It is similar to Tolman's and different from most other CR formulations in that it does not place all of its emphasis on peripheral mediating responses, but allows for the possibility of central perceptual, imaged or other processes utilizing the myriad potential interconnections in the brain. It is different from Tolman in that it conceives of these central processes as obeying the same fundamental laws as overt responses, and hence refers to them as cue-producing "responses."

The central responses, which have been a part of my thinking for a long time, obviously resemble Hebb's (1949) cell assemblies and phase sequences, but in the "go mechanism" and experimental extinction, the present formulation has selective factors which are essential to prevent Hebb's cell assemblies and phase sequences from continuing to grow from association by contiguity until they elicit one grand convulsion.

In short, while certain assumptions of the present tentative formulation necessarily resemble previous theories, I believe that this particular combination of assumptions is unique and that it is precisely this particular combination that actually will work. Certainly, difficulties will be encountered and revisions or extensions will be needed. Only a few lines of further development may be briefly suggested here.

Look for Direct Evidence of "Go" Mechanism

One of the first things that should be done is to try to secure some direct evidence that something like the "go mechanism" outlined in the first assumption actually exists and, if it does, to investigate the degree to which it can be demonstrated to intensify or prolong the activity of neural traces or overt motor activity. What are the effects in different parts of the brain when a given response first gives sudden relief from prolonged pain or causes food to be delivered to a hungry animal which has been thoroughly trained to promptly seize and eat it in the experimental situation? What are the effects during the first trial on which a CS, to which the investigatory response has been habituated, is paired with the UCS of food? We know that after several trials, the CS shows no habituation and that effects of it are more intense and widespread than they otherwise would be. The occurrence of such effects during the very first trial would be evidence for the type of "go" or "booster" mechanism we have postulated. If, however, such effects occurred only on the second trial, this would be evidence for the more conventional conception of a retroactive effect of reward on the strengthening of a connection.

Experimental Tests of Cybernetic Guidance

We also need to know the extent to which drive induction and reduction can cybernetically guide responses as emphasized by Mowrer (1960a). Is such guidance, very effective on the very first trial, or only after S-R connections have been strengthened either by the new process we have just proposed or by some other means? Let us place a rat in an open-field apparatus, wearing a little headlight casting the brightest beam directly ahead. Place a photocell at a given point in the field and have the illumination of this photocell reduce the intensity of electric shock delivered via body electrodes (or electrodes on an aversive area of the brain) placed so that the shock elicits a minimum of interfering motor responses. Will the rat be guided efficiently to that point on the very first trial? Will it be more effective to turn the shock off completely whenever the rat starts to move in the desired direction? If this is done, will the beneficial effects appear only as the strength of the shock is gradually built up again? We need to know more facts about the possibilities, and difficulties, of such guidance as contrasted with learning specific directional responses to specific directional cues.

It seems reasonable to assume that the areas in which Olds (1958) secured self-reward are either a part of the "go mechanism" or are directly connected with it. On the behavioral side, it would be interesting to see whether or not one can guide a rat cybernetically toward a goal by playing "you're getting hotter or colder" with an area in which the animal will hold a bar down continuously in order to get continuous brain stimulation.

The fact that there are so many areas in which the rats do not give themselves continuous stimulation by holding down such a bar continuously, and where they will even perform a second response to turn the stimulation off (Roberts, 1958; Bower & Miller, 1958), poses certain problems for such an experiment, and perhaps also for the hypothesis. Perhaps responses are facilitated, not by the absolute level of activity of the "go system," but only by increases in its level of activity. Perhaps a succession of brief episodes of rises and falls in motivating stimulation will be found to be more effective in cybernetic shaping than continuous feedback.

Relationships between "Go" and "Stop" Mechanisms

While we are clumsily groping along, it is tempting to endow our organism with one or more "stop" mechanisms which have effects directly opposite to those of the "go" one. But this might cause trouble. Desirable as it may be to have pain and fear stop behavior under certain circumstances, as indeed it seems to do in the CER, there are other circumstances, namely escape and avoidance learning, in which it is desirable to have them elicit vigorous activity. The same seems to be true of frustration. Perhaps we might want to have a generalized freezing mechanism with connections from pain and fear that could be strengthened if it was active when their termination activated the "go" mechanism by sudden reductions in pain, fear, and frustration.

Although it does not seem desirable to assume a "stop" mechanism with effects on all responses that are directly opposite to those assumed for the "go" mechanism, it does seem worthwhile to make the following additional assumption which is more tentative than the preceding ones:

7. *That there is a certain amount of reciprocal inhibition between the central mechanisms involved in pain, fear, and frustration and the "go" mechanism, or mechanisms.*

Such inhibition would explain the counterconditioning of fear, which it will be remembered is badly in need of additional detailed experimental study. The activation of the "go" mechanism would tend to inhibit fear, rather than to boost it. The converse aspect of such inhibition would cause pain at the goal to tend to subtract from the effectiveness of reward there. Furthermore, the activation of the "go" mechanism by the termination of pain would be prevented by the inhibiting effects of the pain from being strongly conditioned to cues occurring during the pain. This would account for the apparent difficulty of establishing strong secondary reinforcement based on the termination of pain. (If such secondary reinforcement were strong enough, it could even lead to the performance of responses leading to pain.) The particular responses energized by the termination of pain would not, however, be subject to such inhibition and hence could become anticipatory. Before being too explicit about the inevitability, symmetry, and strength of such reciprocal inhibition, however, it will be wise to have more exact experimental evidence concerning the phenomena to be accounted for. We have already suggested some experiments which might contribute to this goal.

Speed vs. Prepotency

As one tries to apply the hypothesis to a greater variety of situations, problems arise. For example, how can one account for the experiment in which Egger and I (1962) found that, if a first and second cue always are immediately associated with food, the redundant second one has relatively little secondary reinforcing value, and at the same time have the subject take the shortcut of choosing the second cue when subsequently confronted with both simultaneously? A careful analysis of the stimulus changes involved may provide the answer.

Another difficulty arises from the fact that, if rats are specifically rewarded for running slowly down one alley, and allowed to run rapidly down another, they will learn to run at different speeds in the two alleys, but if they are given better rewards for running slowly, they will choose the slow alley (Logan, 1962). In short, the most vigorous response in terms of speed (and presumably amplitude also) is not necessarily the one that is strongest in terms of prepotency. Therefore, we probably shall have to be careful to define strength in terms of prepotency, rather than speed and amplitude.

The lesson is that it is dangerous to regard one hypothesis as more promising than another when it has not been worked out in as much detail. Nevertheless, each hypothesis has to start out in a tentative manner and there is an advantage in trying to work from the general to the specific by a strategy analogous to that employed in the game of "twenty questions."

Changes in Rewards

We know that performance declines when one shifts from a larger reward to a smaller one. Such a decline would be expected if we assume that extinction occurs whenever the CR is stronger than the UCR, or than some given fraction of the UCR.

There is also some disturbance when an animal is shifted from one reward to another, although the laws of such disturbance need to be experimentally determined in more detail, especially since many experiments have confounded shifts in the type of reward with shifts to a less preferred one. We need to find out the extent to which the disturbance is a function of the goal responses elicited by the reward, biting dry food versus lapping sweet water, and the extent to which it can also be produced by distinctive changes in the flavor of food without apparently introducing any change into the motor responses of eating. To what extent do such disturbances become greater as one advances from the rat to the dog to the monkey? Perhaps we shall have to assume a number of "go" mechanisms, or that different strengths of the "go" mechanism function as incompatible responses, or that a conflict between an image and a perceptual response produces a disturbance. In the absence of better data, there is not much point in making overly specific theoretical assumptions.

Furthermore, the problems of sensory preconditioning and latent learning seem to me to be closely related to the foregoing ones.

You will note that in a previous context I said "functioning cues." Having been one of the few stimulus-response psychologists who used the concept of "attention" before our entry into World War II (Miller & Dollard, 1941), I use functioning cues to mean ones that are receiving at least some attention, a concept that has been given a physiological basis by recent work on the reticular formation (Magoun, 1958) and has been extended and clarified by detailed experimental work such as that which Broadbent (1948, 1962) has summarized in support of his filter theory.

Possible Basis for Differences in Intelligence

One possible solution to some of the foregoing problems is to assume that animals with smaller brains, and hence smaller information processing capacity, pay attention to a far narrower range of cues, and perhaps little attention at all to cues that are not associated with rewards for which the animal is motivated (Broadbent, 1962). I believe that my formulation would tend to produce this result.

You will remember that I also have used for over twenty years preceptual and other central responses which get rid of some of the limitations of feedback from purely peripheral anticipatory goal responses (Miller & Dollard, 1941; Miller, 1959). Another more radical solution which is not necessarily incompatible with Broadbent's is to assume that animals with smaller brains and less information handling capacity must use a far larger proportion of that capacity to form "connections" between cues and overt responses, so that perceptual and other central responses play a relatively small role in their behavior. Thus, lower organisms may learn primarily only a certain quantitative conditioned level of the response of the "go system," while higher organisms may learn also more specific and distinctive conditioned images anticipating various sensory aspects of the goal object and its surroundings. Such "responses" could provide a basis for latent learning and for a disturbance produced by changing the goal object. In fact, in higher mammals, the activation of the "go network" may often be mediated by such cue-producing responses.

At the human level, various perceptual expectancies play a great role, but even here some learning occurs in the absence of such expectancies, and under special circumstances behavior may even run counter to them. For example, I once was almost knocked down by an electric shock from a piece of high-voltage electronic equipment. After unplugging it and shorting out the condensors, I was morally convinced that it was impossible to get another shock, reached into the same place, had no conditioned sensory image of an electric shock, but nevertheless felt my hand tend to retract and the hair on the back of my neck to stand up.

SOME ADDITIONAL EXPERIMENTS

Since the main purpose of this paper is to point out some types of experiments which may narrow down the range of possibilities confronting the theorist, it is fitting to conclude it with a few additional suggestions for research.

Is Contiguity Sufficient for Classical Conditioning?

An experiment by Loucks (1935) has been used as an argument against contiguity alone being sufficient for conditioning. He found that following a cue by stimulation of the motor cortex did not establish a CR in dogs. But if the response, lifting the leg, was followed by food when the dog was hungry, conditioning could be established. Recently, however, Doty and Giurgea (1961) have succeeded in establishing CR's by pairing electrical stimulation of a sensory area with that of a motor one. This result suggests that contiguity alone can be sufficient.

Two additional facts should be noted: (1) It is important to distribute the trials rather widely, and (2) the current required is considerably above that needed if the stimulation of the sensory area is used as a discriminative stimulus to elicit a response, such as pressing a bar, motivated by hunger, and rewarded by food (Doty, 1963).

I believe this is an extremely important type of experiment for increasing our understanding about reinforcement. I would like to see further work on the following questions. What are the effects of varying the intensity of the stimulation used as the CS and that used as the UCS? What are the effects of giving food as a reward to a hungry animal immediately after the UCS? Will it serve as a booster "go mechanism" to allow conditioning with weaker stimulation or more massed trials? Such studies will indicate how much weight should be given to the strength of the UCS and how much to a booster effect of reward, and hence be relevant to a more exact formulation of the hypothesis I have just advanced.

Finally, as a check on the conclusion that contiguity alone can be sufficient, I would like to see an extremely rigorous test of the presumed neutrality of the stimulation used by these investigators. First, a dog should be trained to press a bar whenever it is presented, but the rewards for each trial should be on a variable-interval schedule so that the dog will take his time about pressing. Then, with the same spacing between trials that works in the conditioning experiment, the first bar press of each trial should be followed by the same pairing of CS and UCS used in the conditioning experiments. If the speed of this first press is unchanged, these central stimulations are indeed neutral; but speeding up will indicate a rewarding, and slowing down, an aversive effect. This should be a better test than one I have previously proposed (Miller, 1961b).

Investigation of Temporal Factors

Why should the optimum timing of the UCS be approximately 0.5 seconds after the CS? Is this the best timing also for a reward? Is this really the best timing under all circumstances? If so, there must be a fundamental reason. Does reinforcement function best only after certain changes have occurred in the activated neurons, or after certain operations have been performed on the incoming sensory information? If so, we must change our assumptions somewhat so that the "go mechanism" has more effect on "recent traces" than on concurrent responses. Perhaps, as work summarized by Broadbent (1961) indicates, there is a stage of information processing at which only one "chunk" can be reacted to at a time so that the UCS interferes with the CS if the two arrive simultaneously, but not if the CS has already passed this "bottleneck." Perhaps it is an increase in the activation of a response or of a trace which serves as a UCS. We need further evidence before deciding such issues.

On the basis of examining the Russian literature, Razran (1957) concludes that backward conditioning is possible provided the CS is made stronger and the UCS is made weaker. Pavlov (1927) claims that in attempting higher-order conditioning, conditioned inhibition will be established if the new CS and the old one overlap, but that the response may be conditioned to the new one if it is withdrawn before the old one is presented. Can these conclusions be confirmed under a variety of circumstances? If so, they may be important clues to the basic processes involved.

I believe that the Loucks, Giurgea, Doty technique could be used to investigate the foregoing problems because it affords unusually rigorous possibilities for controlling the relevant factors. For example, if electrodes were placed in motor areas to elicit two responses that did not inhibit or facilitate each other too much initially, perhaps one could be used as the "CS" and the other as the "UCS" to investigate simultaneously both forward and backward conditioning as a function of the time-intervals and the relative intensities of stimulation. If a reward will indeed facilitate such conditioning, or if a reward after a response centrally elicited without a CS will cause it to occur to the general situation, a brief powerful stimulation of a central reward area might be used to see whether or not the optimal timing of such a reward is the same as that for a UCS.

Can Stimulation Affect Cultures of Cortical Cells?

Perhaps as Hilgard (1956) has suggested, fundamental advances will depend on finding a peculiarly favorable organism, or artificial modification of an organism, to study. Carrying this idea to its logical extreme—in a way which clearly indicates that it is time to stop this paper—I have been greatly impressed by beautiful motion pictures taken through a microscope of cultures of cortical cells. One sees life and motion in the cells and their endings. What would happen if these cells were subjected to various sorts of stimulation? Could one apply brief episodes of biphasic stimulation to different locations as if they were CS and UCS? Would it be possible to investigate the effects of more chronic electrical or chemical stimulation, and of weak DC potentials or of electrostatic fields? Could we record from such a preparation? Would such studies yield new information about neural growth or learning? I realize that the odds are against this particular wild idea. Perhaps some other idea will be better. We need to exploit fully our increased technical capabilities to open up entirely new lines of investigation of the basic mechanisms of learning.

REFERENCES

Barber, T. X. Physiological effects of "hypnosis." *Psychol. Bull.*, 1961, **58**, 390–419.

Bower, G. H., & Miller, N. E. Effect of amount of reward on strength of approach in an approach-avoidance conflict. *J. comp. physiol. Psychol.*, 1960, **53**, 59–62.

Broadbent, D. E. *Behavior.* New York: Basic Books, 1961.

Broadbent, D. E. *Perception and communication,* New York: Basic Books, 1958.

Brown, J. S. Gradients of approach and avoidance responses and the relation to level of motivation. *J. comp. physiol. Psychol.*, 1948, **41**, 450–465.

Butler, R. A. The effect of deprivation of visual incentives on visual exploration motivation in monkeys. *J. comp. physiol. Psychol.*, 1957, **50**, 177–179.

Bykov, K. M. *The cerebral cortex and the internal organs.* Translated and edited by W. H. Gantt. New York: Chemical Publishing, 1957.

Clark, R., Schuster, C. R., & Brady, J. V. Instrumental conditioning of jugular self-infusion in the Rhesus monkey. *Science*, 1961, **133**, 1829–1830.

Conant, J. B. *On understanding science.* New Haven: Yale Univ. Press, 1947.

Coppock, H. W., & Chambers, R. M. Reinforcement of position prefer-
ence by automatic intravenous injections of glucose. *J. comp. physiol.
Psychol.,* 1954, 47, 355–357.

Delgado, J. M. R., Roberts, W. W., & Miller, N. E. Learning motivated
by electrical stimulation of the brain. *Amer. J. Physiol.,* 1954, 179,
587–593.

Deutsch, J. A. The inadequacy of Hullian derivations of reasoning and
latent learning. *Psychol. Rev.,* 1956, 63, 389–399.

Dollard, J., & Miller, N. E. *Personality and psychotherapy.* New York:
McGraw Hill, 1950.

Doty, R. W., Personal communication, 1963.

Doty, R. W., & Giurgea, C. Conditioned reflexes established by coupling
electrical excitation of two cortical areas. In J. Delafresnaye, A. Fes-
sard & J. Konorski (Eds.), *Brain mechanisms and learning.* London:
Blackwell Scientific Publ., 1961.

Egger, M. D., & Miller, N. E. Secondary reinforcement in rats as a func-
tion of information value and reliability of the stimulus. *J. exp.
Psychol.,* 1962, 64, 97–104.

Egger, D. M., & Miller, N. E. When is reward reinforcing? An experi-
mental study of the information hypothesis. *J. comp. physiol. Psychol.,*
1963, 56, 132–137.

Estes, W. K. Toward a statistical theory of learning. *Psychol. Rev.,* 1950,
57, 94–107.

Fowler, H., & Miller, N. E. Facilitation and inhibition of runway per-
formance by hind- and fore-paw shock of varying intensities. *J. comp.
physiol. Psychol.,* in press.

Fromer, R. The effect of several shock patterns on the acquisition of
the secondary drive of fear. *J. comp. physiol. Psychol.,* 1962, 55,
142–144.

Guthrie, E. R. *The psychology of learning.* (Revised.) New York: Har-
per, 1952.

Harlow, H. F. Learning and satiation of response in intrinsically moti-
vated complex puzzle performance by monkeys. *J. comp. physiol.
Psychol.,* 1950, 43, 289–294.

Harris, L. J., Clay, J., Hargreaves, F. J., & Ward, A. Appetite and choice
of diet. The ability of the vitamin B deficient rat to discriminate
between diets containing and lacking the vitamin. *Proc. Roy. Soc.,*
B113, 1933, 161–190.

Hebb, D. O. *The organization of behavior.* New York: Wiley, 1949.

Hilgard, E. R. *Theories of learning.* (Revised.) New York: Appleton-
Century-Crofts, 1956.

Kimble, G. A. *Hilgard and Marquis' conditioning and learning.* (2nd ed.) New York: Appleton-Century-Crofts, 1961.

Logan, F. A. Conditional-outcome choice behavior in rats. *Psychol. Rev.,* 1962, **69,** 467–476.

Loucks, R. B. The experimental delimitation of neural structures essential for learning: the attempt to condition striped muscle responses with faradization of the sigmoid gyri. *J. Psychol.,* 1935, **1,** 5–44.

MacLean, Paul. John F. Fulton (1899–1960), A midsummer reminiscence, *Yale J. Biol. & Med.,* 1960, **33,** 85–93.

Magoun, H. W. *The waking brain,* Springfield, Ill.: Charles Thomas, 1958.

Meehl, P. E. On the circularity of the law of effect. *Psychol. Bull.,* 1950, **47,** 52–75.

Miller, G. A., Galanter, E., & Pribram, K. H. *Plans and the structure of behavior.* New York: Holt, Rinehart & Winston, 1960.

Miller, N. E. Experimental studies of conflict. In J. McV. Hunt (Ed.), *Personality and the behavior disorders.* New York: Ronald, 1944, 431–465.

Miller, N .E. Learnable drives and rewards. In S. S. Stevens (Ed.), *Handbook of experimental psychology.* New York: Wiley, 1951, 435–572.

Miller, N. E. Drive, drive-reduction and reward. *Proc. 14th Int. Cong. Psychol.* Montreal, June, 1954, 151–152.

Miller, N. E. Experiments on motivation; studies combining psychological, physiological, and pharmacological techniques. *Science,* 1957, **126,** 1271–1278.

Miller, N. E. Liberalization of basic S-R concepts: extensions to conflict behavior, motivation and social learning. *Psychology: a study of a science.* Study 1, vol. 2, S. Koch (Ed.). New York: McGraw Hill, 1959.

Miller, N. E. Some motivational effects of brain stimulation and drugs. *Fed. Proc.,* 1960, **19,** 846–854.

Miller, N. E. Some recent studies of conflict behavior and drugs. *Amer. Psychol.,* 1961, **16,** 12–24. (a)

Miller, N. E. Integration of neurophysiological and behavioral research. *Ann. N. Y. Acad. Sci.,* 1961, **92,** 830–839. (b)

Miller, N. E. Implications for theories of reinforcement. In D. E. Sheer (Ed.), *Electrical stimulation of the brain.* Austin, Texas: Univ. of Texas Press, 1961, 575–581. (c)

Miller, N. E. Analytical studies of drive and reward. *Amer. J. Psychol.,* 1961, **16,** 739–754. (d)

Miller, N. E. Animal experiments on emotionally induced ulcers. *Proc. world congress psychiatry.* Montreal. Vol. III, 1963. (a)

Miller, N. E. Some implications of modern behavior theory for personality change and psychotherapy. P. Worchel & D. Byrne (Eds.) *Personality change.* New York: Wiley, 1963. (b)

Miller, N. E., et al., Graphic communication and the crisis in education. *Audio-visual communication review,* 1957, 5, No. 3.

Miller, N. E., & Dollard, J. *Social learning and imitation.* New Haven: Yale Univ. Press, 1941.

Miller, N. E., & Hart, G. Motivation and reward in learning. Film, Psychological Cinema Register, Penn. State Univ., 1948.

Miller, N. E., & Kessen, M. L. Reward effects of food via stomach fistula compared with those of food via mouth. *J. comp. physiol. Psychol.,* 1952, 45, 550–564.

Milner, B. The memory defect in bilateral hippocampal lesions. *Psychiatric research reports,* 1959, 11, 43–51.

Milner, B. Les troubles de la memore accompagmant des lesions hippocampiques bilaterales. *Physiologie de l'hippocompe,* Colloques Internationaux due centre National de la Recherche Scientifique. No. 107, 275–272, Paris: 1962.

Morrell, F. Electrophysiological contributions to the neural basis of learning. *Physiol. Rev.,* 1961, 41, 443, 494.

Morrell, F. Information storage in nerve cells. In W. S. Fields & W. Abbott (Eds.), *Information storage and neural control.* Springfield, Ill.: Charles C. Thomas, 1963.

Mowrer, O. H. Preparatory set (expectancy) a determinant in motivation and learning. *Psychol. Rev.,* 1938, 45, 62–91.

Mowrer, O. H. On the dual nature of learning—a re-interpretation of "conditioning" and "problem-solving." *Harv. educ. Rev.,* 1947, 17, 102–148.

Mowrer, O. H. *Learning theory and behavior.* New York: Wiley, 1960a.

Mowrer, O. H. *Learning theory and symbolic processes.* New York: Wiley, 1960b.

Mowrer, O. H., & Solomon, L. N. Contiguity vs. drive-reduction in conditioned fear; the proximity and abruptness of drive-reduction. *Amer. J. Psychol.,* 1954, 67, 15–25.

Olds, J. A. Self-stimulation of the brain used to study local effects of hunger, sex, and drugs. *Science,* 1958, 127, 315.

Olds, J. A., & Milner, P. Positive reinforcement produced by electrical stimulation of septal area and other regions of rat brain. *J. comp. physiol. Psychol.,* 1954, 47, 419–427.

Premack, D. Toward empirical behavior laws: I. Positive reinforcement. *Psychol. Rev.,* 1959, 66, 219–233.

Razran, G. The dominance-contiguity theory of the acquisition of classical conditioning. *Psychol. Bull.*, 1957, 54, 1–46.

Roberts, W. W. Both rewarding and punishing effects from stimulation of posterior hypothalamus with same electrode at same intensity. *J. comp. physiol. Psychol.*, 1958, 51, 400–407.

Robinson, B. W., & Mishkin, M. Alimentary responses evoked from forebrain structures in Macaca Mulatta. *Science*, 1962, 136, 260–262.

Rowland, V. *Second conference on brain and behavior*. M. A. B. Brazier (Ed.), in press.

Rusinov, V. S. An electrophysiological analysis of the connecting function in the cerebral cortex in the presence of a dominant area. *Commun. XIX Intern. Physiol. Congr.*, Montreal, 1953.

Shearn, D. W. Does the heart learn? *Psychol. Bull.*, 1961, 58, 452–458.

Sheffield, F. D. A drive-induction theory of reinforcement. Mimeographed MS of paper read at Psychology Colloquium, Brown University, Nov. 1954.

Sheffield, F. D. New evidence on the drive-induction theory of reinforcement. Mimeographed MS of paper read at Psychology Colloquium, Stanford University, Nov., 1960.

Sheffield, F. D., & Roby, T. B. Reward value of a non-nutritive sweet taste. *J. comp. physiol. Psychol.*, 1950, 43, 471–481.

Sheffield, F. D., Roby, T. B., & Campbell, B. A. Drive-reduction versus consummatory behavior as determinants of reinforcement. *J. comp. physiol. Psychol.*, 1954, 47, 349–354.

Sheffield, F. D., Wulff, J. J., & Backer, R. Reward value of copulation without sex drive. *J. comp. physiol. Psychol.*, 1951, 44, 3–8.

Skinner, B. F. *The behavior of organisms*. New York: Appleton-Century-Crofts, 1938.

Smith, M. P., & Capretta, P. J. Effects of drive level and experience on the reward value of saccharine solutions. *J. comp. physiol. Psychol.*, 1956, 49, 553–557.

Solomon, R. L., & Turner, L. H. Discriminative classical conditioning in dogs paralyzed by curare can later control discriminative avoidance responses in the normal state. *Psychol. Rev.*, 1962, 69, 202–221.

Solomon, R. L., & Wynne, L. C. Traumatic avoidance learning: the principles of anxiety conservation and partial irreversibility. *Psychol. Rev.*, 1954, 61, 353–385.

Spence, K. W. *Behavior theory and conditioning*. New Haven: Yale Univ. Press, 1956.

Thorndike, E. L. *The psychology of learning* (Educational Psychology II). New York: Teachers College, 1913.

Thorndike, E. L. A theory of the action of the after effects of a connection upon it. *Psychol. Rev.*, 1933, 40, 434–439.

Tolman, E. C. *Purposive behavior in animals and men.* New York: Appleton-Century-Crofts, 1932.

Weiskrantz, L., & Cowey, A. The aetiology of food reward in monkeys. *Anim. Behav.*, 1963, 11 (in press).

Reinforcement Revisited:
A Structural View

KARL H. PRIBRAM

Stanford University

IN ITS SIMPLEST TERMS, the question that has bothered psychologists is this: An animal learning to solve a problem makes some right movements, some wrong. What is it that reinforces the right ones and discourages the wrong? Why are the right ones remembered in later trials, the rest forgotten? This has been a persistently baffling problem; and its solution is essential to the theory of behavior.

The difficulty may seem trivial. If so, however, the reader may be begging the question by saying to himself in a common-sense (and animistic) way, that the animal of course can *see* that one of his movements has had the right effect, others not. But if the question is asked: What neural processes constitute the "seeing"? the solution is evidently as far off as ever. The simplicity of the question of reinforcement, or selective retention of some responses and not others, is like the simplicity of the fundamental postulates of mathematics that are taking centuries to ravel out [Hebb, 1949, pp. 173–174].

Rewards and punishments; reinforcers and deterrents; successes and failures; utilities and futilities: in one form or another psychologists are concerned with Thorndike's Law of Effect. As

NOTE: This paper and several of the experiments reported have been accomplished with the support of a research career award (MH K6-15214) and a research grant (MH 03732-04) from the National Institutes of Health, Public Health Service; a research contract (DA-49-193-MD-2328) from the United States Army Medical Research and Development Command, and a basic research grant from the Ford Foundation. My thanks are due specifically to Daniel Kimble, Paul McReynolds, Richard Whalen, and Elisabeth Wadleigh, who presented me with the missing links to my thinking at just the moment I needed them. As in any good performance, which I trust this has been, our final thanks go to the "management" for making it all possible.

113

is so often the case when basic conceptions are involved, the picture remains incomplete and clarification is difficult until *neuro*psychological facts are exposed and brought to bear on the problems at issue. And with respect to reinforcement a great deal has already been done. My task today will be to re-examine this body of evidence, add something to it, and propose a view that may reasonably account for it.

First some current definitions and conceptions: (1) a reinforcing event increases the probability of recurrence of a response (Skinner, 1938); (2) reinforcement occurs by contiguity (Estes, 1959; Guthrie, 1942); (3) reinforcement accompanies drive reduction (Hull, 1951; Miller, 1951); (4) reinforcement is related to dissonance reduction (Lawrence & Festinger, 1962); (5) reinforcement informs the organism (Postman, 1953; Tolman, 1932); (6) reinforcement is a warm puppy (Schulz, 1962). These statements range from closely circular descriptions to hedonistic propositions. All are made in good faith by thoughtful and intelligent experimentalists and all have, at one time or another, been voiced in this series of symposia. Hypothesis: they can't all be all wrong in all ways.

A STRUCTURALIST LOOKS AT OPERANT CONDITIONING

"Reinforcement increases the probability of recurrence of a response." This simple definition, proposed by Skinner, has provided an excellent beginning and a steady guide to those who use operant techniques in the study of behavior. Because of its tight circularity, however, the definition leaves something to be desired when the question is asked: What is the neurological process concerned in reinforcement? But even here, experiments of the operant type can fruitfully initiate the inquiry.

Much has been done in this direction. According to the definition, behavior occurs and is followed by a contiguous event. This may be called the outcome or consequence of that behavior (which may be the case or may be acted on by the subject as if it were the case, i.e., as in a superstition). The contiguous event may "shape" the behavior. When this happens, the probability of recurrence of the contiguous response increases (and in many instances the probability of recurrence of other responses in the subject's repertoire in that situation decreases). Whenever this constellation of environment-organism interactions is observed, the event consequent to the behavior is described as reinforcing the behavior. Note that whenever this same constellation of events occurs and the event that increases the probability of recurrence of a response *ante*cedes it, the event is called a discriminative stimulus. One property of reinforcers, therefore, is that they are *consequent* to responses, and are often consequences of actions.

But reinforcing events per se do not affect behavior in a completely predictable fashion. To take an extreme case, one can set up an operant conditioning experiment in such a way that the number of reinforcements obtained during two equal-length testing sessions is the same, though in one the reinforcements are programed according to a fixed ratio, and in the other, according to a fixed interval schedule. The behavior displayed by the organism in these two situations is strikingly different. On the ratio controlled task, the subject shows a continuous, linear, and stable performance curve. Performance controlled by the fixed interval program is cyclical, the curve showing scallop due to a crescendo of activity which reaches a maximum at the moment reinforcement is due. Reinforcements, therefore, have a second important property related to the first: they control behavior through their temporal organization, that is the way they are scheduled or programed. Reinforcers are con*sequences*.

Productive experimental analysis of reinforcement based on the initial definition has been undertaken by David Premack (1959). Premack begins by measuring the rate of a response in a given situation (e.g., the rate of eating) and comparing this rate with another, obtained independently (e.g., the rate of lever pressing per se). He suggests that reinforcement occurs whenever the response with the lower independent rate (lever pressing) coincides, within temporal limits, with the stimuli that govern the occurrance of the response with the higher independent rate (eating). An ingenious set of experiments has been presented in support of this view. One of these is of especial interest (Premack, 1962):

> Parameters were identified for the rat which both made drinking
> more probable than running and running more probable than
> drinking. In the same subjects, depending upon which para-
> meters were used, running reinforced drinking and drinking
> reinforced running. This relationship suggests that a "reward"
> is simply any response that is independently more probable than
> another response [p. 255].

Specifically, an activity wheel equipped with a brake and a
retractable drinkometer were used:

> Drinking contingent upon running was arranged by retracting
> the drinkometer, freeing the wheel and making availability of
> the drinkometer contingent upon running. Conversely, running
> contingent upon drinking was arranged by locking the wheel,
> moving in the drinkometer, and making release of the wheel
> contingent upon drinking [p. 255].

Other instances of such reversals among reinforcers will be
discussed below in relation to the means-ends problem. Here, I
should rather turn to two other matters. First, Premack's experi-
ments and his analysis clearly establish that a response sequence
is reinforcing to the extent that it occurs in the context of
another response sequence (of lower independent rate). This
contextual relationships adds a new and important dimension
to the definition of reinforcement.

Second, Premack discusses only the relation between responses.
He fails to define fully the immediate operations that define
response. Response, in an operant situation, is the indicator of
behavior, the indicator that the organism has acted in and on
the situation. The action includes not only the patterned muscu-
lar contraction (movement) of the organism but the consequences
of that movement. (In fact the response, the indicator of the
action, is one of these consequences.) The response rates studied
by Premack refer not so much, therefore, to the rapidity with
which the movements of the organism take place, but to the
rapidity with which some reliably observed consequences of these
movements can be recorded. For instance, in one set of experi-
ments, a Cebus monkey was used. The monkey might well have
been smacking his lips, circling in the cage, or turning somer-
saults. These were irrelevant movements—and not recorded in
the situation as responses, since manipulation of lever, door,

and bin were the actions under study. And the particular movements involved in these actions are also pretty much irrelevant—the monkey could use his right or left hand, his feet, or even his head to accomplish the response.

What I want to emphasize is that the response, as used in the operant situation, is an indicator of the stimulus aspects of the action—that is, the consequences of that action. Premack's contribution—that response sequences occurring in the context of other response sequences are reinforcing—may thus be more generally restated: reinforcements are *con–sequences* of behavior, that is, event sequences that occur in the context of other event sequences.

THE STRUCTURE OF CONTIGUITY—SOME PSYCHOPHYSIOLOGICAL FACTS

Reinforcement occurs by contiguity. Assuredly, the proponents of togetherness could not mean just this. And yet when one reviews Guthrie and Estes, this is exactly what they mean and hope to mean. Let us listen for a moment to Guthrie: "A stimulus pattern that is acting at the time of response will, if it recurs, tend to produce that response" (Guthrie, 1942, p. 23). Estes' (1958) beautiful analysis, at the 1958 symposium, of the drive-stimulus explanation of drive is certainly in this vein. Guthrie and Estes differ, however, on one point. For Guthrie, "we learn only what we do" (p. 24), and "a student does not learn what was in a lecture or in a book. He learns only what the lecture or book caused him to do" (p. 55). For Guthrie, behavior becomes "its own chief guide" (p. 37) by way of its consequences (movement produced stimuli). For Estes, behavior (i.e., the probability of any response) is guided by sets of stimuli sampled probabilistically, each with its own weight (a parameter determined from the data). However, Estes does not do away with conditions of reinforcement—these "are such that drive cues and experimentally controlled signals will become conditioned (associated) to the same responses" (p. 46). More of this later. Here the point is that we meet contiguity again and again, yet there is a definite difference in emphasis! Guthrie emphasizes response consequences;

Estes, stimulus association. Perhaps in this difference lies the heart of the problem.

What happens when experimentally controlled signals are repetitiously presented to an organism in a constant situation? The organism habituates.

Habituation has received a good deal of attention from neurophysiologists and psychophysiologists recently, with the result that our conception of the process has altered radically. One critical experiment was performed in Moscow by Eugene Sokolov (1960). A tone beep of specified intensity and duration was presented at irregular intervals to a subject whose electroencephalogram, galvanic skin response and plethysmographic record were traced. At the onset of such an experiment characteristic changes in these traces are observed. These accompany behavioral alerting and are known as the orienting reaction. As the experiment proceeds, these indices of orienting become progressively more attenuated until the beep of the tone no longer seems to have any effect. This is habituation. At this point Sokolov reduced the intensity of the tone without changing any of its other characteristics. Immediately the electrical traces from the subject signalled an orienting reaction. Sokolov reasoned, therefore, that habituation could not be simply some type of fatiguing of sensory and neural elements. Rather, a process must be set up in the central nervous system against which incoming sensory signals are matched. Any *change* in signal would result in the orienting reaction. He tested his idea by habituating his subjects anew and then shortening the tone beep. Now the orienting reaction occurred at the moment the shortened beep ended. The electrical traces showed the alerting reactions to the period of *silence*.

These results do not stand alone. For instance, Lettvin et al. (1961) have shown, by use of microelectrodes, that there are nerve cells in the frog's optic lobe that respond by a burst of activity whenever a novel object enters the frog's visual field. The activity of these cells returns to baseline fairly rapidly when the object remains in the field or is repetitiously presented.

There is thus ample evidence for the occurrence of some process in the central nervous system and its appendages against which incoming signals are matched. The process is gradually built up; it may be conceived as a coded representation of prior signals generated by organism-environment interaction; it is subject to alteration by signals of mismatch; (i.e., a partial match); it leads to "expectancies" of the environment by the organism. Such a process has been stated mathematically (Mac-Kay, 1956); its implications for psychology (e.g., in perceptual readiness) have been detailed (Bruner, 1957). Here it is necessary only to point to the facts of the process and to ask what its existence means for the contiguity position.

Contiguity theorists work on the assumption that behavior can be predicated from lawful relations between simultaneously occurring stimulus events and between these and responses. The facts of habituation show that a stimulus event arises from a partial match between a central process and an environmental occurrence. The central process in turn has been formed by the prior occurrence of partial matches between central process and environmental events. Another way of stating this is to say that at any moment in time the central process provides the context in which stimuli arise. Contiguity of stimuli comes to be seen not as some vague "association" but a process occurring as a context-content relationship. And if this is so, stimulus contiguity theory and expectancy theory become brothers under the skin—that is, in the central nervous system.

The question is raised whether the habituation paradigm holds more generally when behavior (that is, responses) is under consideration. Although no answer can now be given, and work is badly needed in this area, the suspicion has been voiced that habituation and extinction have factors in common. For instance, Premack and Collier (1962), in an analysis of the nonreinforcement variables affecting response probability, find it necessary to state that:

> There are at least several reports of unconditioned responses failing to show complete recovery following repeated elicitation. Although the topic has been little investigated, in one of the few pertinent studies, Dodge (1927) reported a partial but apparently irreversible decrement in both latency and magnitude of no less than the unconditioned patellar reflex. Further, the biological literature on habituation contains several cases in which presumably unconditioned responses, having undergone decre-

ment with repeated elicitation, failed to return to initial latency.
... The question is ... whether some degree of irreversible decrement is not more widely characteristic of behavior than is customarily assumed [p. 13].

Let us return to Guthrie and Estes. The emphasis in both the "behavior is its own guide" and the "stimulus sampling" approach must, in the light of these results, begin to stress the importance of the *temporal* organization of contiguity. Organisms do not respond to *any* occurrences that happen simultaneously, contiguously. Their behavior is guided by *stimuli,* including those consequent to behavior. And stimuli are context-determined events, "sampled" on the basis of a central process (a neural "set") determined by *prior* experience and by other central events. An organism's behavior is thus context determined, and is, as well, context determining: response produced events, the outcomes of behavior, consequences, are more than likely (i.e., have a high probability) to partially match a central process and thus act as stimuli—behavior thus becomes its own guide.

In summary, the organization of contiguity is a context-content structure. For the contiguity position, therefore, reinforcements come to be response sequent events occurring in context, that is, con–sequences.

DRIVE STRUCTURES AND THE "REAL" CNS

The most talked about conception of reinforcement is probably the drive-reduction hypothesis. This notion is based on the two-factor theory of drive—that physiological needs set up tensions in the organism (these, as a rule, are manifested in increased general activity); that behavior which reduces such tensions is reinforced. Some have argued (e.g., Sheffield et al., 1955) that organisms seek tension increase—that reinforcement thus accompanies tension increase. This argument does away with the need for the second factor. Drive and reinforcement are still considered covariant, however. Meanwhile, Estes (1958) has convincingly stated the case for a drive-stimulus rather than a drive-tension theory of drive. The question remains, what happens to reinforcement if drive stimuli are conceived to guide behavior directly and not via some tension-state mechanism. A partial answer has been given in the last section: What constitutes a "stimulus" is not as simple as it seems on the surface—that is, external to the organism. But there is much more that can be said. In this area of problems especially, neurologically oriented psychologists have made their mark, and it would be a shame were their work all in vain just because of Estes' lovely analysis. It is not.

First, though, some comments on the organization of a drive-stimulus. This structure is fairly well worked out in many instances. Essentially, it results from the operation of a biased homeostat (Brazier, 1962; Pribram, 1960; Von Euler, 1961). Such an apparatus has a sensitive element—a receptor. Specialized areas sensitive to temperature, osmotic equilibrium, estrogen, glucose, and partial pressure of carbon dioxide are located around the midline ventricular system; these areas are connected to mechanisms which control the intake and output of the agent to which they are sensitive. The areas are embedded in a reticulum (the famous reticular activating systems) which can act to set the level (a bias) at which the sensitive mechanism throws the system into operation. As will become clear, other biases also come to regulate drives. In addition, the entire homeostat is often supplied with secondary, peripherally sensitive mechanisms which aid in the more finely calibred regulations of the agents in question (e.g., to shunt the blood in vessels of the finger tips so as to provide greater cooling or to avoid extreme cooling, on the basis of a blood-finger temperature differential biased by the body's main thermostat).

Still more is known. Electrodes placed in the area sensitive to glucose show an increase in neural activity to occur not when the organism is deprived, but when he has just completed a meal (or has been given intravenous glucose). The idea has been expressed that the activity of the area is proportional to the amount of glucose actively metabolized in the liver. On the other hand, when electrodes are placed in a region lateral to the sensitive area, the converse is found. The activation of the sensitive area inhibits the activity of the lateral region to which it is connected. Whereas destructions around the sensitive mechanism lead to overeating, those in the laterally placed region produce an animal who will not eat at all. And it is the amount of electrical activity that can be recorded from this lateral region that correlates directly with the amount of deprivation of the organism. This region is largely composed of several crossing tracts of fibers in passage—which suggests that the inhibitory effects of the activity of the sensitive area are distributed among several locations in the central nervous system, that is, to the cells of origin of the fibers in question.

But the most striking contribution to the neuropsychology of the drive related theories of reinforcement has not been in the specification of drive stimuli but in producing reinforcement directly with central electrical excitations. Before reviewing these results, however, it becomes advisable to take one more look at the drive-induces-tension, or activation, notion which generated the experiments and has been used in their interpretation. Perhaps I can present my own views on the matter best by using an analogy.

The seashore is a favorite haunt. In northern California, ocean swimming is unfortunately considerably restricted along most of the coast, not only by the recent appearance of sharks but by an extremely dangerous undertow caused by the surf. The beauty of this tremendous, awesome, powerful, cyclical oceanic activity has inspired many (e.g., *The Ninth Wave,* Burdick, 1956). I was therefore particularly impressed one stormy day while flying, to observe a peaceful coastal scene composed in part by series of stable, standing wave patterns. Could it be that those who concern themselves with drive solely as activation fail to see its structure because they maintain too close a view of the particular data they wish to describe? If this is so, a more complete encompass should, without denying the validity of the narrower set of problems, be able to include them in the wider formulation. And having said this, perhaps it will be possible to take the longer view without losing the feel of excitement and turbulence of participation in the storm-blown scene below. Be that as it may, the distinction, recently succinctly presented by Roger Brown (1962), between homeostatic and drive (i.e., tension) theories will come up more and more frequently in the next sections.

Olds and Milner (1954) discovered that an animal would

press a lever in order to electrically excite certain parts of its brain. In his presentation in this series of symposia, Olds (1955) distinguished between physiological need, drive, reward, and punishment, and stated that the last three might all covary, or that any two might, or that each might require separate treatment. His own view was that reward and punishment were probably separable and that each would have a drive component. For Olds, physiological needs were drive stimuli; drive resulted in general activity of the organism; reward and punishment served as response selectors.

More recently, Deutsch (1960) has examined the self-stimulation effect in the light of his own theory, which also demands separation of drive and reinforcement (i.e., reward and punishment) factors. In Deutsch's theory, drive is directly derived from need and therefore can be equated with Estes' and Olds' drive stimuli. However, in the Deutsch mechanism, excitation derived from drive-stimuli and that derived from reinforcing stimuli (initiated in peripherally located receptors) are apt to display different properties.

He has made good use of this presumed difference. In a recent series of studies, he has clearly manipulated the self-stimulation effect in such a way as to produce "drive" effects that are different from "reinforcement" effects. These have been recently reviewed (Deutsch & Howarth, in press). Essentially, three sets of ingenious experiments are reported: (1) extinction of lever pressing and maze running was found to be a function of time from the last brain excitation, and not of the number of *un*reinforced lever presses or maze runs; (2) extinction of lever pressing (and maze running) was found to be delayed or interrupted by interposing conditions that would "normally" produce lever pressing (or maze running) e.g., by an aversive stimulus; (3) extinction was delayed by low voltage or low frequency, but hastened by high voltage or high frequency trains of excitation, administered to the electrode independent of response. These results show that the central nervous system referents of drive and reinforcing events can be separately manipulated—that any exclusive definition of one in terms of the other (as in the drive related theories) is difficult to maintain.

What then *is* the relation between reinforcement and drive? Deutsch suggests that afferent excitation derived from peripheral sensory receptors converges on a neural "link" which has already been connected to the drive stimulus. Another way of stating this is that the reinforcing event acts on a neural mechanism preset by the drive stimulus. M. D. Egger and Neal Miller (1963) have recently reported a series of experiments which they interpret in somewhat similar terms: the reinforcing event gives information about the drive state. In both statements the drive structure is conceived to preset the organism—to provide the context within which the reinforcing events are to operate.

Drive, structured as a biased homeostat, thus serves in turn as the bias or setting for the consequences of behavior. These, as will be described in the following section, have a structure of their own—a structure not dissimilar to that of the biased homeostat. For the present, it suffices to make clear that the drive structure can, and does in the experiments cited, bias the consequences of behavior.

But there is more. To turn again to the nervous system, Olds, in his presentation to this series of symposia (1955), detailed the anatomical systems of the forebrain from which self-stimulation could be obtained in his hands. These structures, formally called rhinencephalic, have become more widely known as the limbic areas since their relation to olfaction is relatively limited. Olds reviews the evidence:

> As we mentioned earlier anatomical and physiological evidence can be cited to indicate that structures related closely or remotely to olfaction are divided into three systems: System I has direct connection with the olfactory bulb. It contains none of the structures we have discussed. System II including septal area and some amygdaloid nuclei, is connected with system I but not with the olfactory bulb. Further, it is related to the anterior hypothalamus. This system has been implicated in diverse functions: olfactory, gustatory, metabolic, socioemotional.
>
> Finally, system III is defined by having connections to system II but none to the first system or to the olfactory bulb. It includes the hippocampus, and the cingulate gyrus; and it is connected anatomically to the posterior hypothalamus and the anterior thalamus.
>
> Now, the interesting fact is that our Skinner box tests, which

were not even conceived when Pribram and Kruger (1954) classified limbic structures, validate the distinction between second and third system [pp. 120–121].

The validation to which Olds refers is that the rate of lever pressing increased over 50 per cent when electrodes were implanted in system II; when the implant location was system III rates increased from 20–32 per cent. No endbrain stimulations in locations other than these reliably gave an increase in response rate—of eighty-six electrode placements there were only two (one on the edge of the lateral geniculate nucleus, the other in the white matter of the cerebrum) from which a spurious increase in response rate occurred, and this sporadically (not every day). I have reviewed eleswhere (Pribram, 1960) in considerable detail the evidence that concerns the presumed functions of these limbic systems. This evidence need not, therefore, be restated here. The generalization suggested from the review, relevant here, was that these systems function in an especial way in the execution of behavior sequences, particularly those involved in feeding, fleeing, fighting, mating, and maternal behavior. This portion of the review concludes:

> Analysis of the neural mechanism that underlies the execution of sequences of actions has just begun. Electrical changes have been recorded from the amygdaloid complex of the limbic systems whenever the organism is exposed to a novel event or one that has meaning in terms of reward and punishment (Grastyan, 1959; John & Killam, 1959). These electrical changes subside once the organism is familiar with the event unless the hippocampal formation of the limbic systems has been ablated, in which case electrical changes continue to occur when this or any other event takes place. The amygdaloid complex is necessary to the establishment of electrocortical conditioned responses. The suggestion has been made that the hippocampal formation inhibits (perhaps by way of the reticular core of the brain stem) the succession of unrelated inputs to the amygdala that might occur and so allows this structure to maintain the neural activity necessary to the conditioning process. In a conditioning or learning situation, electrical changes are recorded from the hippocampal formation during the initial trials; later, no such changes accompany successful action; they occur only when errors are made (Adey, 1959) [Pribram, 1960, pp. 13–14].

Currently, the evidence continues to accrue. Kimble (1963) compared the behavior of rats who had had the hippocampus removed bilaterally with that of isocortically operated and unoperated control groups. He showed an increase for the "hippocampal" group in repetitive running in an open field situation; poorer performance of these subjects on a successive brightness discrimination task; and a greater number of errors in Hebb-Williams mazes.

> Qualitative differences between the hippocampal Ss and the other two groups were also observed. The hippocampal Ss initially ran rapidly along the perimeter of the open field, stopping only rarely. They typically traversed the interior of the field only after 2–5 min. The most striking characteristic of their behavior was an extremely repetitive running pattern. The behavior of the other two groups differed radically from that of the hippocampal group. It consisted of "bursts" and "stops." A typical performance was to run to one wall, explore around the perimeter of the field once or twice, stop and groom, stand up on the hind legs and sniff, run out into the center of the field, explore in a seemingly random fashion, and return to a corner for more grooming and occasional crouching [p. 274].

Subsequently Kimble has gone on to examine more directly the effect of hippocampal removals (Fig. 1), this time in monkeys. For this he made use of a new automated discrimination apparatus (DADTA). This allows ready trial by trial computational analysis of performance (Figs. 2 & 3) (Pribram et al., 1962). Groups of monkeys were trained on (1) a simple visual discrimation task; (2) two types of sequential tasks, in one of which the order of "correct" choice was completely predetermined, while in the other "incorrect" choice was limited to those occasions where the animal chose a cue repetitiously; and (3) discrimination tasks in which trials were spaced from five seconds to six minutes. No difference between a "hippocampal"group of four subjects and operated controls appeared in the performance of any of the discriminations (tasks 1 & 3) (Fig. 4); the hippocampal group was, however, markedly defective (Figs. 5 & 6) in the performance of both sequential tasks (Kimble & Pribram, 1963).

Interestingly, improved performance could be obtained if the consequences of each panel press were accentuated by dim-

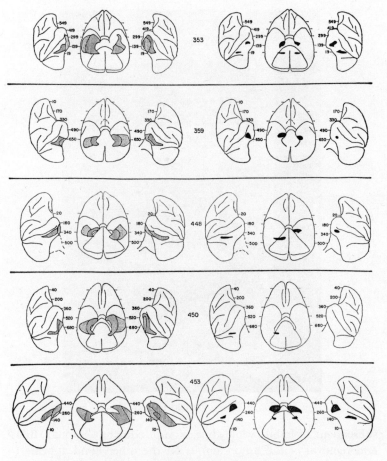

Fig. 1.

ming the "houselight" in the test cage. Both the control subjects and those with hippocampal lesions showed improvement—that of the hippocampal group sent their performance above the chance level.

Habituation and dishabituation (orienting) is also affected by limbic lesions (Kimble & Bagshaw, unpublished data). Amygdalectomy markedly reduces the number of galvanic skin responses to a novel stimulus. The time-course of habituation and

Fig. 2.

subsequent dishabituation appears approximately normal. Bilateral removal of the hippocampus on the other hand appears to alter only dishabituation (Kimble & Bagshaw, unpublished data). The first change in stimulus conditions produces no reaction; a subsequent change, however, results in a marked increase in the number of galvanic skin responses, at least double that of the controls. This lowered reactivity to the initial change may account for the failure to perform the behavior sequences unless each consequent event is doubly signaled.

Now it remains to be shown how the results of these experiments on behavior sequences and habituation relate to those that have demonstrated reinforcement by way of self-stimu-

Fig. 3.

lation of limbic formations. Again, a suggestion has come from the laboratory.

Ross Adey (1960) has studied the electrical activity that can be recorded from the hippocampal formation of cats during learning of a simple visual discrimination task. Very careful but complicated analysis has led him to venture that the phase relations between wave patterns recorded from the deeper and the more superficial portions of the hippocampal cortex change as a function of task performance. Early, while many errors are made, the activity recorded from the deeper layers of the hippocampal cortex precedes that from the more superficial layers; later, when performance contains many error-free runs, the reverse is the case. Input to the deeper layers is from other core structures of the brain; input to the more superficial layers is from the adjacent entorhinal and cingulate cortex.

Despite the preliminary nature which this datum must have because of the state of the computing art in neurobiological science, it nonetheless strikes a responsive chord. This is especially so since Flynn, MacLean, and Kim (1961) had concluded in their

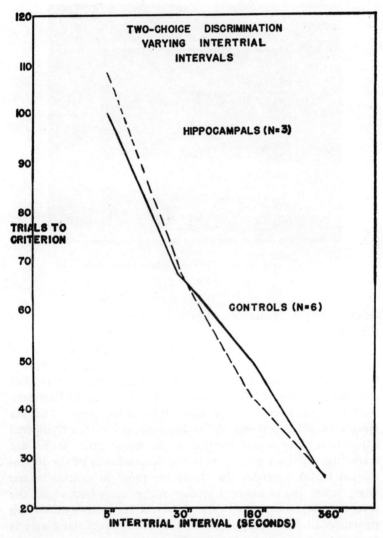

Fig. 4.

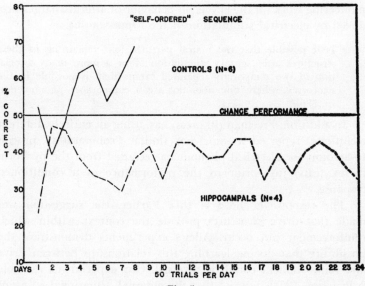

Fig. 5.

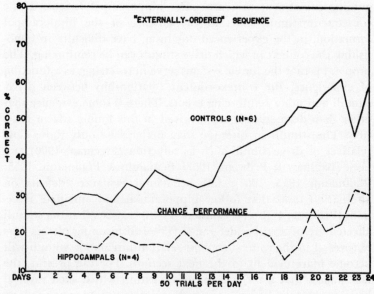

Fig.6.

pioneering work on the effects on behavior of afterdischarges produced by electrical stimulation of the hippocampus:

> Is it possible that the neural perturbations remaining in these structures after sensory stimulation allow a more ready association of two temporally separated events than is possible in the neocortex, where one does not see a comparable phenomenon [p. 386]?

In addition, Freeman (in press) has, using an entirely different technique, reported a somewhat similar "comparator" process to account for electrical phenomena recorded from the pyriform cortex (cats) just prior to the performance of a conditioned response.

The responsive chord is this. Earlier, the suggestion was made that drive structures provide the context within which reinforcement can occur. Adey's experiments demonstrate the possibility that during learning this relationship between drive and reinforcement could be reversed. Our experiments (Kimble & Pribram, 1963) indicate that the external, situational stimulus events consequent to behavior are considerably less effective in guiding subsequent responses after hippocampal lesions. These consequent stimuli may, in the absence of the hippocampal formation, in the experienced organism, have difficulty in establishing the context in which drive stimuli can be reinforcing. The proposal is that the limbic systems serve in reversing, as a function of experience, the context-content relationship between drive-stimuli and other reinforcing events. There is some evidence that other than drive-stimuli are involved in this limbic system function. The stimuli in question may perhaps be only those close relatives of drive-stimuli such as olfaction (Freeman, 1960) and taste (Bagshaw & Pribram, 1953; Benjamin & Pfaffmann, 1955; Pfaffmann, 1955, 1961); but behavioral evidence (deficits on alternation tasks that follow hippocampal and cingulate resections [Pribram, Wilson & Connors, 1962]) suggests that the stimuli affected are of a still wider range. The full meaning of this type of reversal in the context-content relationship among stimuli will become more evident in the next sections. For the present, the fact suffices that a mechanism exists within which such reversal between drive and external stimuli is demonstrated to take place.

To summarize: (1) The neural structure of a drive-stimulus is a biased homeostat. (2) Electrical self-stimulation has been shown to be analyzable into at least two components: one probably related to drive stimuli, the other to reinforcement. (3) The limbic systems of the forebrain, prominent loci from which the electrical self-stimulation effect is obtained, are also essential to the proper performance of behavior sequences. (4) Some evidence is at hand that these systems make possible the juxtaposition of two sets or classes of inputs. These certainly include the neural consequences of drive stimuli, and the neural consequences of actions on experimentally arranged task stimuli—but there is also evidence (e.g., Schwartzbaum & Pribram, 1960) that the juxtaposition of any two sets of experimentally arranged stimuli (as in a transfer of training task) may also be accomplished through the office of limbic system mechanisms. (5) The analysis of the electrical concomitants of task performance suggests that such juxtaposition is effected through a "comparison" mechanism, not through a blending (or simple compounding) of signals. (6) Apparently, a reversal of precedence of stimulus events occurs as a function of learning. This suggests that a reversal of the context-content relationship among stimulus sets is effected and is reminiscent of Premack's experiment on the reversal between the reinforcing role of drinking and running. (7) On this basis, the suggestion is made that the outcomes of actions initially biased *by* drive stimuli can, through experience, come *to* bias them. Apparently, the brain behaves truly as it must, if sequences of events in the context of other sequences of events, guide behavior; that is, if consequences reinforce.

PERFORMANCE THEORY: ADDICTIONANCE AND EFFECTANCE

But there is more to the problem of reinforcement than to meet the concerns of drive theorists. This past year, Lawrence & Festinger (1962) have made an important contribution: faced with an impasse in the learning theory derived from animal experiments, they have made a statement about rat behavior in the context of a theory designed to cope with the behavior of man.

The impasse is this: response strength, that is, the probability that a response should recur, ought to be, according to learning theory, proportional to the occurrence and immediacy of appropriate reward and inversely related to the effort expended to obtain that reward.

> Recently, there has accumulated a considerable body of experimental evidence suggesting that these common assumptions underlying learning theory fail to give an adequate description of changes in response strength. In fact, there is the suggestion that under some circumstances the variables of reward, temporal delay, and effort may have just the opposite effects from those predicted by the assumptions . . . [p. 6]

This impasse is not a new one for those working in a physiological orientation. Miller, Bailey, & Stevenson (1950) found that the lesions of the ventromedial region of the hypothalamus which produce the syndrome of hypothalamic hyperphagia (overeating) do *not* induce the subject to work more for food; on the contrary, these animals will work *less* than their controls under similar conditions of deprivation. The conditions that determine this dissociation have been fully explored (e.g., Teitelbaum & Epstein, 1962). In another series of experiments, performed in our laboratories, the variables that determine the response sequence displayed in the "fixed interval" reinforcement situation were analyzed. Over-all rate of response, dependent on deprivation, was found to be sensitive to limbic system lesions, but the distribution of per cent of responses in a "scallop" was unaltered by either deprivation or limbic area destructions. Frontal isocortical lesions, on the other hand, altered the "scallop" without changing over-all rate of response (or, for that matter, the rate of reinforcement).

The evidence to which Lawrence and Festinger address themselves, however, concerns what happens during extinction. In essence, the more the effort, and the fewer and more delayed the rewards, the slower the learning, but the more resistant the behavior will be to extinction. In operant situations, behavior established under conditions of continuous reinforcement extinguishes almost immediately; behavior established under conditions of variable schedules of reinforcement is more resistant to alterations of scheduling.

In their experimental and logical analysis, Lawrence and Festinger dispose of several prior explanations forwarded to resolve this impasse. The resistance to extinction cannot be simply conceived as dependent on a failure in discrimination, an insufficiency of information, or the development of competing responses. Rather, they propose that, when "competing," "incongruent," "dissonant" sets of information are supplied to the organism, its behavior persists beyond the point expected if either set were alone operative: an animal that, during a non-choice situation, experiences a set of conditions that he is shown to choose *less* frequently in a free-choice situation, will show increased resistance to extinction. In man, the "dissonant" state is stated to arise when two cognitions, that is, two sets of information, would suggest two different actions. Most of the body of experiment and, I believe, much of the spirit of the argument, is concerned with the state aroused when such dissonant sets occur *in sequence*. For instance, dissonance is aroused when the result of taking some action does not lead to consequences which sufficiently "justify" the action taken. If the set of information consequent to the action were available beforehand, and choice were free, the action would not have been undertaken. Another way of stating this is to say that expectations were not met by consequences—that antecedent and reinforcing events do not match—that dissonance results from this mismatch.

Dissonance reduction can come about in two ways: (1) the organism "can convert the consequences of the act into something that 'justifies the action'" or (2) it "can change its behavior so that it becomes consonant with the consequence experienced (e.g., the animal may, during extinction, refuse to run, provided this does not lead to consequences still more dissonant). The question remains as to what consequences "justify" action (Lawrence & Festinger's "extra attractions") and what it means to say that behavior "becomes consonant with the consequences experienced."

A few observations are in order. It is common knowledge among morphine addicts that very often the strength of the addiction is proportional to the amount of "hustling" that is required to obtain the drug. In fact, in most cases, patients who have had prolonged morphine therapy and who go through withdrawal symptoms when treatment is discontinued, have an (understandable) aversion to the drug and addiction is not a particularly severe problem. Recent experiments with rhesus monkeys suggest that the situation is not much different here (Clark & Polish, 1960; Clark, Schuster, and Brady, 1961). ("Personality" variables, of course, play a considerable role; yet the over-all observation holds sufficiently to affect the laws regulating morphine distribution, e.g., in the British Isles.) The similarity to the dissonance producing paradigm is unmistakable (thus the term "addictionance" theory). And the observation thus leaves us with the same unsettled and unsettling questions.

Could it be that activity per se is rewarding? This makes little sense, for it would not account for the difference between, say, "hustling" and unordered, random hyperactivity. And here we may have a clue: Could it be that *ordered* activity per se is rewarding? And again, what can be meant by "ordered activity"? —certainly not patterned muscular contractions, since these are equally manifest when we observe random activity. No, clearly, when the *consequences* of action become orderly, consonant, that is, sequences appearing *in context,* then and only then is activity ("judged") rewarding, that is, reinforcing.

Support for this view comes from another quarter. Mace (1961) has called attention to the fact that, in an affluent society, man and beast tend to reverse the means-end relationship.

> What happens when a man, or for that matter an animal, has no need to work for a living? . . . the simplest case is that of the domesticated cat—a paradigm of affluent living more extreme than that of the horse or the cow. All the basic needs of a domesticated cat are provided for almost before they are expressed. It is protected against danger and inclement weather. Its food is there before it is hungry or thirsty. What then does it do? How does it pass its time?
>
> We might expect that having taken its food in a perfunctory way it would curl up on its cushion and sleep until faint internal stimulation gave some information of the need for another perfunctory meal. But no, it does not just sleep. It prowls the garden and the woods killing young birds and mice. It *enjoys* life in its own way. The fact that life can be enjoyed, and is most enjoyed, by many living beings in the state of affluence

(as defined) draws attention to the dramatic change that occurs in the working of the organic machinery at a certain stage of the evolutionary process. *This is the reversal of the means-end relation in behavior.* In the state of nature the cat must kill to live. In the state of affluence it lives to kill. This happens with men. When men have no need to work for a living there are broadly only two things left to them to do. They can "play" and they can cultivate the arts. These are their two ways of enjoying life. It is true that many men work because they enjoy it, but in this case "work" has changed its meaning. It has become a form of "play." "Play" is characteristically an activity which is engaged in for its own sake—without concern for utility or any further end. "Work" is characteristically activity in which effort is directed to the production of some utility in the simplest and easiest way. Hence the importance of ergonomics and work study—the objective of which is to reduce difficulty and save time. In play the activity is often directed to attaining a pointless objective in a difficult way, as when a golfer, using curious instruments, guides a small ball into a not much larger hole from remote distances and in the face of obstructions deliberately designed to make the operation as difficult as may be. This involves the reversal of the means-end relation. The "end"—getting the ball into the hole—is set up as a *means* to the new end, the real end, the enjoyment of difficult activity for its own sake [pp. 10–11].

A somewhat similar statement has been presented during this series of symposia by Robert W. White (1960). He emphasizes the role played by the progressive achievement of competence in the maintenance of behavior, and makes a strong case that the "feeling of efficacy" is an important guide to behavior.

Effectance is to be conceived as a neurogenic motive, in contrast to a viscerogenic one. It can be informally described as what the sensory-neuro-muscular system wants to do when it is not occupied with homeostatic business. Its adaptive significance lies in its promotion of spare-time behavior that leads to an extensive growth of competence, well beyond what could be learned in connection with drive-reduction [p. 103].

White is concerned with the implications of effectance in clinical psychology; here our concern is with what the sensory-neuro-muscular system "wants."

According to the foregoing analysis, the common problem for dissonance theory, addiction theory, means-end theory, and effectance theory is that activities of a certain type appear to be self-maintaining in the face of situations which in a drive-reduction frame of reference would be predicted to extinguish the behavior. In the previous section, the relation between drive and reinforcement was shown to be one of sequentially occurring events set in context (context provided either by the drive-stimuli or the environmental stimuli, "comparison" taking place in the limbic systems). In the present section, the relation between action and reinforcement has been found to be somewhat similar—in the case of action, however, the consequences of the actions must provide their own set within which a subsequent event will be consequent—that is, reinforcing.

In many respects, what has been discussed in the latter half of this section is the development of behavior differentiation—that is, skill. Effectance and competence, play and gamesmanship, demand precise timing of actions within larger sequences of actions, so that consequences—sequences in context—will form a harmonious production. And a great deal is known about the neurology of skill. Here, perhaps, more than anywhere else, the model of "sequence in context" can be realized in tissue—and, in fact, the model was originally devised to handle some new neurological facts in this area [Miller, Galanter & Pribram, 1960].

At the reflex level, control of muscular contraction can no longer be conceived simply in terms of the reflex arc (some excitation of receptors, transmission of the signal aroused by such excitation to the central nervous system, and back again to the muscle in question). The change in conception is necessitated by the discovery that the activity of the γ efferent fibers, fibers that transmit signals from the central nervous system to the receptors in the muscle (muscle spindles), acts as a feedback, that is, controls the amount of activity recordable from the afferents that signal the state of the receptor to the central nervous system. The presence of this feedback loop makes it difficult at any moment in time to assess the origin of a particular amount of activity in the afferent nerves, and thus the state of the receptor. That state could reflect the state of contraction (isomorphic or isotonic) of its muscle group or it could reflect the amount of activity of the γ efferent system, or both. Only a comparison between states at successive moments, in the context of γ efferent activity, will give a signal of the state of contraction of the muscle group. The γ efferent activity provides the setting, the context, the bias on the muscle receptor. (On occasion, the reverse may well be the case. The bias may be set by the muscle contraction and changes in γ efferent activity computed.) The feedback model, very similar to the biased homeostat, applies, therefore, not only to behaviors where drive stimuli are involved, but also to behaviors where the consequences of muscular contractions per se are under consideration.

Sherrington, in his classic lectures on the Integrative Action of the Nervous System (1906), was not unaware of the problem, and his statement of it is worth repeating (though his solution is cast in simple associative terms—reinforcement for Sherrington occurs through immediate spinal induction [summation through increased intensity and coextensity of convergent inputs]):

> We note an orderly sequence of actions in the movement of animals, even in cases where every observer admits that the coordination is merely reflex. We see one act succeed another without confusion. Yet, tracing this sequence to its external causes, we recognize that the usual thing in nature is not for one exciting stimulus to begin immediately after another ceases, but for an array of environmental agents acting concurrently on the animal at any moment to exhibit correlative change in regard to it, so that one or other group of them becomes—generally by increase in intensity—temporarily prepotent. Thus here dominates now this group, now that group in turn. It may happen that one stimulus ceases coincidently as another begins, but as a rule one stimulus overlaps another in regard to time. *Thus each reflex breaks in upon a condition of relative equilibrium, which latter is itself reflex.* In the simultaneous correlation of reflexes some reflexes combine harmoniously, being reactions that mutually reinforce [p. 120; italics supplied].

At the cerebral level, also, neurology has a great deal to say about skill. Removals of the precentral "motor" cortex of primates (including man) certainly results in awkward performance (Pribram et al., 1955–56). Equally disruptive are lesions of the cerebellar hemispheres, those portions of the cerebellum that are directly connected with the precentral cortex through the ventrolateral portion of the dorsal thalamus. The functional relationship between precentral cortex and cerebellum has been the subject of considerable work. An overbrief summary runs as in the following paragraph.

Each part of the precentral motor cortex controls the muscles, movements and action of a portion of the body. This part of the cortex also receives a direct input from the portion it controls. In addition, this same portion receives an input via the cerebellum. The assumption has been that a match between these inputs is made and that the signal resulting from this match activates the pyramidal tract through which muscle control is effected. And there is ample evidence to support the assumption. Awkwardness due to cerebellar lesions results in "intention tremor"—smooth performance is converted to a jerky sequence (almost as if a biased homeostatic mechanism were thrown into oscillation). And the effect of precentral cortex removals has been suggested to be a change in facilitation of reflex actions—in some experiments, disinhibition resulting in spasticity (Denny-Brown, 1948), in others, defacilitation (Lashley, 1924).

The suggestion is that the organization of action resembles the biased homeostat, the structure of drives. It follows that the bias of the neural mechanisms in control of action should be resettable, much as is the bias of the drive homeostats to produce the phenomenon of self-stimulation. This has been accomplished by John Lilly (1959). Prolonged trains of excitation (subliminal to those that would produce movement) were delivered to the precentral motor cortex whenever the lever was depressed by the subject (a monkey). Lever pressing had to be paced so that the on-off nature of the excitation could be maintained. The monkey learned to do this, however, and spent many (may I say "happy"?) hours at this occupation.

Obviously, the interrelations among the neural systems that regulate skilled, highly differentiated action are complex. It may be that careful perusal of the literature and a few critical experimental results could make out a clear hierarchical arrangement among systems in such a way that each locus of match between inputs serves as a setting within which the occurring events must operate. This is not the place for such an extensive analysis. It suffices to pose the problem and to point out in summary, that a neural mechanism does exist whereby order can be achieved among actions and their consequences—again the brain is as it must be, since skilled behavior is possible.

This has been a long way from dissonance to effectance to skill. The point is simply that these areas of interest pose a common problem: how is it that selective behavior is maintained in the absence of guides from drive stimuli—or, in the extreme, when behavior apparently goes in a direction contrary to one plausibly related to drive stimuli? The suggestion made in this section is that the consequences of actions are truly stimulus events that occur in sequence and that, once some order has been initiated in this sequence of stimuli, this order per se can provide the set or context for the occurrence of the next or sub-sequent event. Actions have consequences and the consequences of actions are reinforcers. Behavior, thus, becomes its own guide.

PERCEPTUAL PERFORMANCES: REINFORCEMENT AS INFORMATION PROCESSING

Would that this were all there need be said about reinforcement. But in 1960 I offered the suggestion that reinforcement is "the reverse of the coin of similarity" and, of course, many others, including Tolman (1932) and Postman (1953) in his contribution to this group of papers, have conceived of reinforcement as information. According to the hypothesis which guides this presentation, "we couldn't all have been all that wrong." Let me review the statement:

> But perhaps the model has its greatest power in the description of what constitutes reinforcement for the organism. The posterior intrinsic mechanism, because of the hierarchical nature of its selective control over its own modification, allows a change in the representation to occur by trial and error. Whenever the error signal is such that the corrective change is not uniquely specified, the representation is modified to include this information, and trials continue. Thus an organism that possesses this mechanism can, given a relatively unchanging or slowly changing environment, search that environment for the additional information that is needed to make the organism fully informed. The neural model would thus account for the search through negative instances

as these are defined in the stimulus-sampling type of stochastic learning theories (Bush & Mostellar, 1951; Estes, 1950, 1955; Green, 1958), search by an information-hungry organism reinforced or satisfied only when corrective change of the representation is immediate and can be deduced uniquely from the error signal. Stated in this way, reinforcement becomes one side of the coin of similarity [Pribram, 1960, p. 18]!

There I was concerned with what Bruner (1957) has called perceptual readiness and Postman calls the arousal of perceptual response dispositions (1953, p. 86). Here I have been discussing reinforcement in relation to learning and to performance theories. Perhaps in this distinction lies the key to some of the problems that have remained puzzling.

The concept "reinforcement" was spawned by learning theory to account for the fact that performance-change is effected through consequences of actions as well as by the cues in a situation. The set of problems presented in the last section came to light when an impasse in learning theory was encountered. Facts of performance failed to fit the facts of learning in any simple fashion. However, as was shown, the concept "reinforcement" continued to be a useful one and did not need redefinition. The laws that govern the operation of reinforcing events in this area of problems are apparently somewhat different from those derived in classical learning theory—a distinction is therefore in order: *performance theory* might well encompass this body of data.

A somewhat similar smudging of distinctions has taken place in perceptual theory. Hebb (1949) and Postman (1953) are both initially responsible and many others have fallen in with the current vogue in talking about perceptual learning. Should it turn out that the definition of reinforcement which has served thus far holds for perceptual theory as well, this could clear the air. The element common to all three areas would be established and the reason for treating them together, exposed. This would then allow renewed effort in the direction of specifying differences between them: for assuredly perception, performance (behavior differentiation), and learning (behavior change) do have some elements to distinguish them.

To return for a moment to performance theory. Lawrence and Festinger point out that one way the organism responds to dissonance is to seek "extra attractions" to maintain the behavior. I have made the case that such "extra attractions" can result from the consequences of the actions themselves, provided they have an opportunity to become progressively orderly: that behavior differentiation can become "the extra attraction." Lawrence and Festinger, I am sure, would not want to be limited to this mode of dissonance reduction. The fact that they speak of dissonant "cognitions" suggests that in a situation, any set of events that can be progressively ordered might serve as well. And these events could arise in the receptors by which the organism engages his environment, that is, the events could be perceptual.

The evidence that perceptual differentiation takes place need not be reviewed here. The work of the Gibsons (1955) is well known, as are Hebb's (1949), Piaget's (1955), Postman's (1953), and Bruner's (1958) contributions. I should rather address myself to two questions: (1) is the concept of reinforcement tenable in this area of problems; and (2) what is the connection between progressive differentiation, hierarchy, and the model of the biased homeostat?

If reinforcement is conceived as a consequence of action, what is the action involved in perceiving? Operant conditioning has admitted "looking responses" to the repertoire. Looking certainly involves muscular contractions—the muscles of the eye must move it to make and maintain contact with the exciting energy. Focusing the retinal image also involves the muscles of accommodation. In hearing, the muscles of the middle ear have been shown important to the process of habituation in this modality. And sniffing is certainly a part of perceiving olfactory cues. Further, the experiments of Ivo Köhler (in press) and of Held (Held & Hein, 1958; Held & Schlank, 1959) have shown that perceptual performance depends in good part on more general performance experience in the situation. Finally, there is the well-known fact that passive pushing of the eyeball leads to blurring of vision, while active movement "presets" the perceptual mehcanism in such a way that vision is possible. Evidence of this sort has been collated by Teuber (1960) and given a theoretical base. A somewhat similar model for the process has recently also been detailed by MacKay (1957 a, b; 1958 a, b). And the model is essentially the model of reinforcement with which we are concerned (Pribram, 1960). The consequences of looking must involve events subsequent to context—context active in the movement of the eye. This context must be some self-adapting error-sensitive mechanism that has control over its own input; in other words, a biased, settable, homeostatic-like structure. However, I need not detail anew such a model here. Floyd Allport (1955), after his classic, critical and comprehensive review of theories in perception, was led by his analysis to propose the outlines of a structural model. Let us look in on his event-structure theory of perception:

> The first step of the theory is the conceptualization of a complete and potentially repetitive cycle of ongoings and events. . . . Both these effects [positive interaction and inhibitory interaction between cycles] might be present in one . . . system, as in the principle of negative feedback, if the main line production is also considered as a cycle. . . .
>
> We now proceed to a further step. The closed chain of ongoings and events, since it is neither open-ended nor indefinitely extended in space, but a real (cyclical) entity, can be used as a unit of a structure of a larger or "compounded" type. . . . The total structure is the "including" structure. . . . In other words we can build a "higher order" of structure made up of a cycle of cycles of ongoings and events. Still higher orders can be structured as cycles of these larger cycles, and so on. This development of the model will be called the property of "order." It should now be noted that the principle of ordering is not 'limited to event-cycles; it can apply also to event-systems [pp. 635–636].

Allport presented his theory of event-structure as a way of looking at the problems of perception—not as a definitive theory. The similarities of his view to those expressed in the past two sections leaves little doubt that event-structures in perceptual theory, and reinforcement (viewed structurally) in learning and in performance, have many essential properties in common. I should like to believe, in fact, that event-structure and the mechanism of reinforcement are structurally identical. So conceived, event-structuring is a process through which the consequences of perceptual acts (e.g., looking) become ordered, much as this ordering takes place in the development of skills. Perceptual problems can, in this light, be approached as if they were sensory performances. Differences between motor (i.e., instrumental) and sensory performances would quickly show themselves—for sense organs and the striped musculature of the organism are differently related to their environment.

But it remains now to be shown that the neural organization of sensory performance partakes of the properties assigned to reinforcing events. In discussing the structure of contiguity, the facts of the orienting reaction to "novel" stimuli and of habituation were presented. Is there any direct evidence that these processes take place in a neural mechanism closely connected to sense-organ function? There is. Lettvin et al. (1961) describe the following reactions of cells in the frog's optic tectum:

> *"Newness" neurons:* These cells have receptive fields about 30 degrees in diameter.... They are distributed so as to map continuously the visual field with much overlap. Such a neuron responds a little to sharp changes in illumination. If an object moves across the receptive field, there is a response whose frequency depends on the jerkiness, velocity, and direction of the movement, as well as on the size of the object. There is never an enduring response [p. 773].
>
> *"Sameness" neurons:* Let us begin with an empty gray hemisphere for the visual field. There is usually no response of the cell to turning on and off the illumination. It is silent. We bring in a small dark object, say 1 to 2 degrees in diameter, and at a certain point in its travel, almost anywhere in the field, the cell suddenly "notices" it. Thereafter, wherever that object is moved it is tracked by the cell. Every time it moves, with even the faintest jerk, there is a burst of impulses that dies down to a mutter that continues as long as the object is visible. If the object is kept moving, the bursts signal discontinuities in the movement, such as the turning of corners, reversals, and so forth, and these bursts occur against a continuous background mutter that tells us the object is visible to the cell.
>
> When the target is removed, the discharge dies down. If the target is kept absolutely stationary for about two minutes, the mutter also disappears. Then one can sneak the target around a bit, slowly, and produce no response, until the cell "notices" it again and locks on [p. 774].

My interest in "perceptual readiness" and a model that would account for it stems from the results of a series of neuro-behavioral experiments. Some years ago, in our analysis of the functions of the posterior "association" cortex of monkey, our group discovered (cotemporaneously with Harlow [1953]) an area on the inferolateral surface of temporal lobe that functions in vision (Blum, Chow, & Pribram, 1950). Additional work showed that lesions in this locus disturbed visual behavior only—somesthetic, taste, and auditory functions could be assigned elsewhere. Further, all sorts of visual choice behaviors were disrupted: choices among colors, patterns, objects, luminances were equally affected, provided the task was equally difficult (number of trials to learn) for unoperated, normal monkeys (Pribram, 1954). Finally, vision was not affected if *choice* was not involved: the monkey could groom, pick a gnat out of midair, and gauge his rate of lever pressing according to the level of illumination in a "ganz-field" (Ettlinger, 1959).The variables that influence choice were also investigated: stimulus object similarity (Mishkin & Hall, 1955) and factors influencing response difficulty (Pribram & Mishkin, 1955) were found important. But in a test of the effect of varying the number of alternatives in the situation an interesting fact came to light. The performance difficulty of the lesioned monkeys was related not to the number of alternatives in the situation but to the number of alternatives sampled—the lesioned group of monkeys consistently made their choices from among a smaller set of stimulus objects than did the control subjects (Pribram, 1959).

The anatomical relations of this inferolateral portion of the temporal lobe are also of interest. There is no specifically visual input to this area as far as is known today. The area is three neurons removed from the striate optic-cortex—and no further away from the auditory cortex of the supratemporal plane, and not much further, neuronwise, for that matter, from the postcentral somatosensory areas. Also, severance of the connections between striate and inferolateral cortex by circumsection of the occipital lobe fails to affect visual choice behavior. On the other hand, there is an efferent tract that arises both in the occipital and inferolateral temporal cortex and ends in the neighborhood

of the superior colliculus—an important structure in the visual
mechanism which, among other things, has to do with the regu-
lation of eye movements. The real possibility exists, therefore,
that the restricted sampling and related effects on visual choice
behavior produced by inferolateral temporal lobe lesions are due
to a defect produced in the presetting of the visual mechanism:
a defect in the process of establishing the context within which a
subsequent event can become consequent, that is, reinforcing.

Enough has been said to show that reinforcement viewed as a
structure has use in the area of perceptual theory. There remains
another problem, however, which has been repeatedly touched
upon but which, so far, has been only vaguely formulated: namely
the relation between a cyclic, homeostatic-like process and pro-
gressive differentiation. Homeostats can be hierarchically ar-
ranged. The blower on the home-furnace of a hot-air system
is controlled by a thermostat separate from, but subordinate to,
the main thermostat. There is some evidence that the food
appetitive and general activity mechanisms of the organism are
both contained within the larger regulation of basal temperature
(Brobeck, 1945, 1948, in press). But, I believe, this simple state-
ment of a hierarchical relationship does not give a full account
of the progressive differentiation process which is of concern
here. What seems to happen in performance differentiation and
in perceptual differentiation is a true reversal of means and
ends; of context and content; of bias and the mechanism biased.
Differentiation can take place in the biases placed on the
mechanism—the temperature of a home will be controlled by
several thermostats, each of which biases the main mechanism
but is in turn biased by it. This complex yet orderly interrelation
among subsystems and system achieves stabilities beyond those
possible for the simpler systems. The suggestion is that the biased
homeostat becomes differentiated, mainly through differentia-
tion of its bias, perhaps because of inherent imperfections. These
imperfections must be in the control the mechanism has over
the variables to which it is sensitive. This poses a paradox—for
differentiation occurs most readily when such control appears
to be accomplished. But just at these junctures, increased sensi-
tivity is also achieved: namely, the thermostatic system that has

allowed temperature to vary between 65 and 75 degrees Fahrenheit is insensitive to temperature changes of 1 or 2 degrees. When the system is sufficiently stable to control temperature at 70 degrees it becomes exquisitely sensitive to a 2 degree change. And these new sensitivities cause the system to react where it would not have on prior occasions. Thus, though this is a structural, even a homeostatic, view of the behavioral process, its design certainly does not lead to stagnation.

Much remains to be done in the way of clarification of the neural mechanisms involved in such a cyclic process that leads to perceptual (and behavioral) differentiation. But the problem is stated: According to the view put forward here, perceptual and performance differentiation occurs since biased homeostatic processes—mechanisms of reinforcement—continually operate to achieve stability. Once control of a certain order has been momentarily established, new sensitivities within the context of the old appear, and these in turn must be dealt with: that is, these new (novel) events become the consequences of the behavior—the events sequent and in context—the reinforcers.

The Anatomy of Happiness

The theme is reinforcement. Each of the preceding sections is a variation on that theme, that variation produced by a set of techniques and problems. In this section I hope to draw out the theme itself more fully.

Reinforcements are considered con–sequences of instrumental, motor, and sensory acts—event sequences that occur in the context of other event sequences. The model of event structure presented is the biased homeostat, a feedback unit which has the capacity to differentiate. This model has been spelled out in a variety of ways: one way is as a set of test-operate–test-exit units, hierarchically organized into a branching program or Plan, suggested by George Miller, Eugene Galanter, and myself (1960). This formulation has the advantage of analogy with computer information processing, so that problems generated can be tested by hardware as well as software operations.

The suggestion has also been made that under some circumstances reinforcing events function as biases on feedback units, homeostats. Further, differentiation of performance and of perception has been attributed to the differentiation of this bias mechanism, the reinforcing process. Is there any direct support for equating reinforcement and bias? I believe there is.

Whalen (1961) has used a situation similar to that already described in which drive and reinforcing stimuli were teased apart. In Whalen's experiment, reinforcement resulted not from electrical self-stimulation of the brain, but by sexual activity. Whalen showed that the choice between two alleys of a maze depends on the occurrence of an intromission, but running speed in the maze increases with the number of such occurrences.

Spence (1955, p. 127–148) has reported a similar result when pellets of food are used as reinforcers. These results are congruous with Miller's (already mentioned) proposal that choice—and the rate of learning of that choice—depend simply on the information given by the reinforcing event. But Whalen's and Spence's results demonstrate that, once performance is established, reinforcing events display another property: namely, an increase in the number of reinforcements causes performance rate to increase monotonically (over a range). Another way of stating this effect on performance is to say that reinforcers place a value on the performance—reinforcement biases the performance.

In *Plans and the Structure of Behavior* (Miller, Galanter, & Pribram, 1960) we discussed two aspects of motivation: Plan and Value. Plan clearly directs performance, that is, Plans program choices. Value played some other, less well-specified role in the initiation and the "seeing through" of Plans. When Value is stated to be a bias on performance (and of course, this includes perceptual performance), a clearer conception is attained.

However, another problem is immediately raised. If reinforcements bias performance, place values on them, how are reinforcers then informative? The solution to this problem lies again in the reversal of the context-content relationship. When, during learning, reinforcements give information they must operate, by the definition of the term information, within a set or bias already established. When, on the other hand, reinforcements bias performance, they establish the set within which other events become informative. Thus the consequences of actions and perceptions are informative *or* valuative according to whether they take place within another context or they themselves serve as the context.

Some of the conditions that govern the occurrence of context-content reversals have been detailed in each of the earlier sections. Much more could have been added. When mechanisms of drive serve as context, utility theory applies: preferences form the contextual matrix within which the consequences (outcomes) of actions and perceptions are informing. When, due to affluence, the means-ends reversal has taken place, "futility" and performance theory must take over—the consequences of action become the context within which other consequences, drive, and perceptual stimuli give information about the gamesmanship or skill. And when perceptual stimuli provide the context, values are recognized to bias the operation of both drives and actions.

But, perhaps more important would be a summary of the similarities and differences between the structure of reinforcement proposed here and the conceptions of others working in each of the areas covered by a section:

Experimentalists working in the tradition of operant conditioning have pointed the way to a descriptive definition of reinforcement and have demonstrated the reversibility of the response relationships that result in reinforcement. However, the distinction has been blurred between a "response" as an indicator of action and a "consequence" of an action conceived as a stimulus event. This blurring has led to the possible confusion that reinforcement is composed by the concatenation of muscular events. Once consequences of actions are seen for what they are— stimulus sequences that occur in the context of other stimulus sequences—the confusion is no longer possible.

Contiguity theorists have depended heavily on the simple idea that stimulus events, whether of muscular, extero- or interoceptive origin, must somehow come into contact in order to guide behavior. This faith has been amply rewarded, not only by their own work at the behavioral level, but by neurophysiologists who have detailed the loci and systems where such contact occurs. Neurophysiology and psychophysiology have gone a step further, however. It turns out that what constitutes a stimulus event is itself a contiguity affair. A stimulus is seen to result *only* when there is a partial match between some coded neural representation of prior inputs to the organism (or some innately operating mechanism awaiting "release"). A stimulus thus is shown to arise by contiguity, that is, within the context of some already established process. Contiguity becomes a context-content relationship among stimulus sets, *temporally* ordered. And so theoretical distinctions between contiguity and expectancy theory vanish. A reinforcing event is any consequence of behavior that alters the context-content relationship, that is, any consequent stimulus. The proposal here presented should allow better specification of what constitutes a stimulus (reinforcing or otherwise) by those who hold the contiguity position—perhaps the central problem for their theory and for behavior theory in general.

Drive theorists have been concerned primarily with physiological need-produced tension states. Estes' analysis cleared the air considerably by demonstrating that many of the problems faced could be solved by considering drives as stimuli. The neuropsychological work presented here takes this analysis a step further. Drive stimuli are seen to arise from the operation of homeostats, which control the production of the physical or chemical substances to which they are sensitive. The level at which these mechanisms become sensitive can, within limits, be set, that is, biased. Self-stimulation by electrical currents delivered to the brain was suggested to operate by setting this bias. But the regions of the endbrain, the limbic systems, from which self-stimulation is obtained, do not deal only with drive-stimuli. In later sections of the paper, the structure of action-produced stimuli and even perceptual structure was shown to be similar to the structure of drives—that is, to biased homeostats. And reversals among these several classes of potentially contextual structures were shown to be impaired when lesions are made in the limbic systems. Reinforcers, the consequences of action, were shown to become, on the basis of experience, the bias or context within which a drive stimulus is informing where, initially, the set of drive-stimuli were the context within which the reinforcing event informed.

Activation, the concept of tension, was not completely done away with, however. As detailed in the section on perception, homeostats, even biased ones, are imprecise, faulty mechanisms. In a relatively constant environment, however, they manage to become progressively adapted—that is, they stabilize the inputs to their sensitivities. Once this is accomplished, however, they are also more sensitive to smaller perturbations in these inputs and so new problems of stabilization arise. The suggestion is made that one mechanism for achieving stability and therefore sensitivity is the differentiation of the bias—more homeostats are brought to bear on the input. These homeostats must, however, be interconnected, that is, each biased by the other, to achieve a maximum of control. Again, as this level of control is achieved, new sensitivities develop and new mechanisms differentiate to cope with them. A structural view of this sequence of operations shows it to be that of a biased homeostat; a closer view, however, would discern a cyclic pattern of coping followed by control and new sensitivity—and another cycle of coping. The coping phase might well be called activation, since neural and behavior unrest would characterize this phase.

For the rest, this proposal, by focussing on reinforcement, makes possible a view of dissonance, addiction and effectance as performances which need not necessarily follow the laws established for learning by behavior theory. In the same fashion, "perceptual learning" is unravelled: the clear statement of what reinforces perceptions may allow perceptual theory to return to other matters. And, what may be even more important, reinforcement is seen to be a part of a stimulus event-structure irrespective of the receptor of origin of the stimuli: problems in the domain, "motivation," can be stated in terms familiar to those working in perception.

A final thought. Pfaffmann (1960) has stated the case for the pleasures of sensation elegantly. Perhaps *this* paper has brought us a bit closer to understanding happiness. Classically, happiness is conceived as "entelechy," that is, "self-actualization" (Maslow, 1955) and not hedonistically. Cyclically recurring phases have been described to characterize achievement (Toman, 1960; Erikson, 1962): during each cycle, progressively more control is gained over a set of events; when this control reaches a certain level, new sensitivities develop. Then satiety sets in, reorganization (of context-content relationships?) takes place, and the cycle starts afresh. This cyclic process is, of course, most clearly apparent in behavior related to physiological needs. There is some evidence that feeding and sexual satiety are accompanied by marked activation of the electrical patterns recorded from the brain, and especially from limbic structures, despite the fact that behaviorally the organism is asleep (Sawyer, in press). These "paradoxical sleep records" are similar to those obtained when man dreams during sleep (Jouvet, 1961; Dement, in press). In fact, persons routinely awakened whenever the paradoxical sleep waves appear, fail to feel rested after sleeping.

The suggestion is that happiness is slowly achieved through the progressive gain in control over stimulus events, through the structuring of con–sequent performances, that is, through reinforcement. In the course of human existence, many moments recur when control reaches the point, just before the reorganization of satiety, when sensitivity is maximal. At such moments, "happiness is a warm puppy."

REFERENCES

Adey, W. R. Presentation at symposium on the rhinencephalon. Amer. Acad. Neurol., April 17, 1959.

Adey, W. R., Dunlop, C. W., & Hendrix, C. E. Hippocampal slow-waves; distribution and phase relations in the course of approach learning. *A.M.A. Arch. Neurol.*, 1960, 3, 96–112.

Allport, F. A. *Theories of perception and the concept of structure.* New York: Wiley, 1955.

Bagshaw, M. H., & Pribram, K. H. Cortical organization in gustation (macacca mulatta). *J. Neurophysiol.*, 1953, 16, 499–508.

Benjamin, R. M., & Pfaffmann, C. Cortical localization of taste in the rat. *J. Neurophysiol.*, 1955, 18, 56–64.

Blum, Josephine, Chow, K. L., & Pribram, K. H. A behavioral analysis of the organization of the parieto-temporo-preoccipital cortex. *J. comp. Neurol.*, 1950, 93, 53–100.

Brazier, M. A. B. (Ed.) *Brain and behavior,* proceedings of the Second Conference. Los Angeles, February 1962, in press.

Brobeck, J. R. Effects of variations in activity, food intake and environmental temperature on weight gain in the albino rat. *Amer. J. Physiol.*, 1945, 143, 1–5.

Brobeck, J. R. Food intake as a mechanism of temperature regulation. *Yale J. Biol. & Med.*, 1948, 20, 545–552.

Brobeck, J. R. In M. A. B. Brazier (Ed.), *Brain and behavior*, proceedings of the Second Conference. Los Angeles, 1962, in press.

Brown, R. Models of attitude change. In *New directions in psychology*. New York: Holt, Rinehart & Winston, 1962. Pp. 1–85.

Bruner, J. S. On perceptual readiness. *Psychol. Rev.*, 1957, 64, 123–152.

Bruner, J. S. Neural mechanisms of perception. In *Brain and human behavior*, Ass. res. nerv. ment. Dis., 1958. Pp. 118–143.

Burdick, E. *The ninth wave*. Boston: Houghton Mifflin, 1956.

Bush, R. R., & Mostellar, F. A model for stimulus generalization and discrimination. *Psychol. Rev.*, 1951, 58, 413–423.

Clark, R., & Polish, E. Avoidance conditioning and alcohol consumption in rhesus monkeys. *Science*, 1960, 132, 223–224.

Clark, R., Schuster, C., & Brady, J. Instrumental conditioning of jugular self-infusion in the rhesus monkey. *Science*, 1961, 133, 1829–1830.

Dement, W. Eye movements during sleep. In M. Bender (Ed.), *The ocular motor system*, USPHS symposium on ocular motor system, April, 1961, in press.

Denny-Brown, D., & Botterell, E. The motor functions of the agranular frontal cortex. *Res. publ. ass. nerv. ment. Dis.*, 1948, 27, 235–345.

Deutsch, J. A. *The structural basis of behavior*. Chicago: Univ. of Chicago Press, 1960.

Deutsch, J. A., & Howarth, C. I. Some tests of a theory of intracranial self-stimulation. *Psychol. Rev.*, in press.

Dodge, R. *Elementary conditions of human variability*. New York: Columbia Univ. Press, 1927.

Egger, M. D., & Miller, N. E. When is a reward reinforcing: an experimental study of the information hypothesis. *J. comp. physiol. Psychol.*, 1963, 56, 132–137.

Erikson, E. H. The roots of virtue. In Sir Julian Huxley (Ed.), *The humanist frame*. New York: Harper & Row, 1962.

Estes, W. K. Toward a statistical theory of learning. *Psychol. Rev.*, 1950, 57, 94–107.

Estes, W. K. Theory of elementary predictive behavior: an exercise in the behavioral interpretation of a mathematical model. In *Mathematical models of human behavior—proceedings of a symposium*. Stamford, Conn.: Dunlap & Associates, 1955.

Estes, W. K. Stimulus-response theory of drive. In M. R. Jones (Ed.), *Nebraska symposium on motivation, 1958.* Lincoln: Univ. of Nebraska Press, 1958. Pp. 35–68.

Estes, W. K. The statistical approach to learning theory. In S. Koch (Ed.), *Psychology: a study of a science.* Vol. 2. New York: McGraw-Hill, 1959. 380–491.

Ettlinger, G. Visual discrimination with a single manipulandum following temporal ablations in the monkey. *Quart. J. exp. Psychol.,* 1959, 11, 164–174.

Freeman, W. J. Correlation of electrical activity of prepyriform cortex and behavior in cat. *J. Neurophysiol.,* 1960, 23, 111–131.

Freeman, W. J. The electrical activity of a primary sensory cortex—analysis of EEG waves. *Int. rev. Neurobiol.,* 1963, 5, in press.

Flynn, J. P., MacLean, P. D., & Kim, C. Effects of hippocampal after discharges on conditioned responses. In D. E. Sheer (Ed.), *Electrical stimulation of the brain; an interdisciplinary survey of neurobehavioral systems.* Austin: Univ. of Texas Press, 1961. Pp. 380–386.

Gibson, J. J., & Gibson, E. J. Perceptual learning: differentiation or enrichment. *Psychol. Rev.,* 1955, 62, 32–41.

Grastyan, E. In M. A. B. Brazier (Ed.), *The central nervous system and behavior, transactions of the second conference.* Josiah Macy, Jr., Foundation, 1959.

Green, E. J. A simplified model for stimulus discrimination. *Psychol. Rev.,* 1958, 65, 56–63.

Guthrie, E. R. Conditioning: a theory of learning in terms of stimulus, response, and association. In National Society for the Study of Education, *The forty-first yearbook.* Bloomington, Ill.: Public School Publ. Co., 1942.

Harlow, H. F. Higher function of the nervous system. *Ann. Rev. Psychol.,* 1953, 15, 493–514.

Hebb, D. O. *The organization of behavior; a neuropsychological theory.* New York: Wiley, 1949.

Held, R., & Hein, A. V. Adaptation of disarranged hand-eye coordination contingent upon re-afferent stimulation. *Percept. & Motor Skills,* 1958, 8, 87–90.

Held, R., & Schlank, M. Adaptation to disarranged eye-hand coordination in the distance dimension. *Amer. J. Psychol.,* 1959, 72, (4), 603–605.

Hull, C. L. *Essentials of behavior.* New Haven: Yale Univ. Press, 1951.

John, E. R., & Killam, K. F. Electrophysiological correlates of avoidance conditioning in the cat. *J. pharm. exp. Therap.,* 1959, 125, 252–274.

Jouvet, M. Recherche sur le mechanisme neurophysiologique du sommeil et de l'apprentissage negatif. In *Brain mechanisms and learning.* Oxford: Blackwell, 1961. Pp. 445–479.

Kimble, D. P. The effects of bilateral hippocampal lesions in rats. *J. comp. physiol. Psychol.,* 1963, 56, 273–283.

Kimble, D. P., & Pribram, K. H. Hippocampectomy and behavior sequences. *Science,* 1963, 139, 824–825.

Köhler, I. Development and alterations of the perceptual world. In G. Klein (Ed.), *Psychological issues,* in press.

Lashley, K. S. Studies of cerebral function in learning. V. the retention of motor habits after destruction of the so-called motor areas in primates. *Arch. Neurol. Psychiat.,* 1924, 12, 249–276.

Lawrence, D. H., & Festinger, L. *Deterrents and reinforcement: the psychology of insufficient reward.* Stanford, Calif.: Stanford Univ. Press, 1962.

Lettvin, J. Y., Maturana, H. R., Pitts, W. H., & McCulloch, W. S. Two remarks on the visual system of the frog. In W. A. Rosenblith (Ed.), *Sensory communication*—Contributions to the Symposium on Principles of Sensory Communication, 1959, M.I.T. New York: The M.I.T. Press & John Wiley & Sons, 1961. Pp. 757–776.

Lilly, J. C. In M. A. B. Brazier (Ed.), *The central nervous system and behavior, transactions of the First Conference.* Josiah Macy, Jr., Foundation. Madison, N. J.: Madison Printing Co., 1959. P. 276.

Mace, C. A. Psychology and aesthetics. *Brit. J. Aesthetics,* 1962, 2, 3–16.

MacKay, D. M. The epistemological problem for automata. In *Automata studies.* Princeton, N. J.: Princeton Univ. Press, 1956. Pp. 235–252.

MacKay, D. M. Moving visual images produced by regular stationary patterns. *Nature,* 1957, 180, 849–850. (a)

MacKay, D. M. Some further visual phenomena associated with regular patterned stimulation. *Nature,* 1957, 180, 1145–1146. (b)

MacKay, D. M. Moving visual images produced by regular stationary patterns. *Nature,* 1958, 181, 362–363. (a)

MacKay, D. M. Perceptual stability of a stroboscopically lit visual field containing self-luminous objects. *Nature,* 1958, 181, 507–508. (b)

Maslow, A. Deficiency motivation and growth motivation. In M. R. Jones (Ed.), *Nebraska symposium on motivation, 1955.* Lincoln: Univ. of Nebraska Press, 1955. Pp. 1–30.

Miller, G. A., Galanter, E., & Pribram, K. H. *Plans and the structure of behavior.* New York: Henry Holt & Co., 1960.

Miller, N. E. Learnable drives and rewards. In S. S. Stevens (Ed.), *Hand-*

book of experimental psychology. New York: Wiley, 1951. Pp. 435–472.

Miller, N. E., Bailey, C. J., & Stevenson, J. A. Decreased "hunger" but increased food intake resulting from hypothalamic lesions. *Science,* 1950, 112, 256–259.

Mishkin, M., & Hall, Martha. Discriminations along a size continuum following ablation of the inferior temporal convexity in monkeys. *J. comp. physiol. Psychol.,* 1955, 48, 97–101.

Olds, J. Physiological mechanisms of reward. In M. R. Jones (Ed.), *Nebraska symposium on motivation, 1955.* Lincoln: Univ. of Nebraska Press, 1955. Pp. 73–138.

Olds, J., & Milner, P. Positive reinforcement produced by electrical stimulation of septal area and other regions of rat brain. *J. comp. physiol. Psychol.,* 1954, 47, 419–427.

Pfaffmann, C. Gustatory nerve impulses in rat, cat, and rabbit. *J. Neurophysiol.,* 1955, 18, 429–440.

Pfaffmann, C. The pleasures of sensation. *Psychol. Rev.,* 1960, 67, 253–268.

Pfaffmann, C. The sensory and motivating properties of the sense of taste. In M. R. Jones (Ed.), *Nebraska symposium on motivation, 1961.* Lincoln: Univ. of Nebraska Press, 1961. Pp. 71–108.

Piaget, J. *The language and thought of the child.* (Marjorie Gabain, Trans.) New York: Noonday Press, 1955. Ch. 5. Pp. 171–240.

Postman, L. The experimental analysis of motivational factors in perception. In *Current theory and research in motivation: a symposium.* Lincoln: Univ. of Nebraska Press, 1953. Pp. 59–108.

Premack, D. Toward empirical behavior laws. I. Positive reinforcement. *Psychol Rev.,* 1959, 66, 219–233.

Premack, D. Reversibility of the reinforcement relation. *Science,* 1962, 136, 255–257.

Premack, D., & Collier, G. Analysis of nonreinforcement variables affecting response probability. *Psychol. Monogr.,* 1962, 76 (5).

Pribram, H. W. Toward a science of neuropsychology (Method and data). In *Current trends in psychology and the behavioral sciences.* Pittsburgh: Univ. of Pittsburgh Press, 1954. Pp. 115–142.

Pribram, K. H. On the neurology of thinking. *Behav. Sci.,* 1959, 4, 265–287.

Pribram, K. H. A review of theory in physiological psychology. In *Ann. Rev. Psychol.* Palo Alto, Calif.: Annual Reviews, Inc., 1960, 11, 1–40.

Pribram, K. H., Gardner, K. W., Pressman, G. L., & Bagshaw, Muriel.

An automated discrimination apparatus for discrete trial analysis (DADTA). *Psychol. Reports,* 1962, 11, 247–250.

Pribram, K. H., & Kruger, L. Functions of the "olfactory brain." *Ann. N. Y. Acad. Sci.,* 1954, 58, 109–138.

Pribram, K. H., Kruger, L., Robinson, F., & Berman, A. J. The effects of precentral lesions on the behavior of monkeys. *Yale J. Biol. & Med.,* 1955–56, 28, 428–443.

Pribram, K. H., & Mishkin, M. Simultaneous and successive visual discrimination by monkeys with inferotemporal lesions. *J. comp. physiol. Psychol.,* 1955, 48, 198–202.

Pribram, K. H., Wilson, W. A., & Connors, Jane. The effects of lesions of the medial forebrain on alternation behavior of rhesus monkeys. *Exper. Neurol.,* 1962, 6, 36–47.

Sawyer, C. H. Presentation at third conference on brain and behavior. Los Angeles, February 1963, in press.

Schulz, C. M. *Happiness is a warm puppy.* San Francisco: Determined Productions, Inc., 1962.

Schwartzbaum, J. S., & Pribram, K. H. The effects of amygdalectomy in monkeys on transposition along a brightness continuum. *J. comp. physiol. Psychol.,* 1960, 53, 396–399.

Sheffield, F. D., Wulff, J. J., & Backer, R. Reward value of copulation without sex drive reduction. *J. comp. physiol. Psychol.,* 1955, 48, 387–391.

Sherrington, C. *The integrative action of the nervous system.* New Haven: Yale Univ. Press, 1947. (1906)

Skinner, B. F. *The behavior of organisms: an experimental analysis.* New York: Appleton-Century-Crofts, 1938.

Sokolov, E. N. In M. A. B. Brazier (Ed.), *The central nervous system and behavior, transactions of the third conference.* Josiah Macy, Jr., Foundation, 1960.

Spence, K. W. *Behavior theory and conditioning.* New Haven: Yale Univ. Press, 1956.

Teitelbaum, P., & Epstein, A. The lateral hypothalamic syndrome: recovery of feeding and drinking after lateral hypothalamic lesions. *Psychol. Rev.,* 1962, 69, 74–90.

Teuber, H. L. Perception. In *Handbook of physiology, sect. 1: neurophysiology.* Vol. 3. Baltimore: Waverly Press, 1960. Pp. 1595–1668.

Tolman, E. C. *Purposive behavior in animals and men.* New York: Appleton-Century-Crofts, 1932.

Toman, W. On the periodicity of motivation. In M. R. Jones (Ed.),

Nebraska symposium on motivation, 1960. Lincoln: Univ. of Nebraska Press, 1960. Pp. 80–95.

Von Euler, C. Physiology and pharmacology of temperature regulation. *Pharmacological Rev.*, 1961, 13, 361–397.

Whalen, R. E. Effects of mounting without intromission and intromission without ejaculation on sexual behavior and maze learning. *J. comp. physiol. Psychol.*, 1961, 54, 409–415.

White, R. W. Competence and the psychosexual stages of development. In M. R. Jones (Ed.), *Nebraska symposium on motivation, 1960*. Lincoln: Univ. of Nebraska Press, 1960. Pp. 97–140.

Central Neural Inhibition

H. W. MAGOUN

Brain Research Institute and
University of California

IN THE REMARKABLY FINE series of presentations on motivation
which have been presented at the University of Nebraska over
the past decade, it is desirable at some point to devote attention
to the central neural influences which reduce or prevent, rather
than promote or increase behavior. The need for consideration of
inhibitory as well as excitatory processes in psychological think-
ing has recently been elaborated by Diamond, Balvin, and Dia-
mond (1963), and the present account will attempt to survey
contributions to knowledge of the stop, rather than the go mech-
anisms of the brain. While emphasis will be placed on the elec-
trophysiological observations on which current advances chiefly
rest, whenever possible their related significance for behavior will
be explored. After reference to the appropriateness of such a pre-
sentation in this Sechenov Centennial Year, consideration will
proceed from focal to generalized reduction of central neural
function, in sequential discussion of external inhibition, habitua-
tion, internal inhibition, light sleep, and deep sleep.

CENTRAL NEURAL INHIBITION

Just a century ago, a young medical graduate from Moscow,
named Sechenov, spent the winter of 1862 in Claude Bernard's
laboratory in Paris in research upon the frog. He induced the
spinal withdrawal reflex, and then excited the animal's brain by
applying crystals of salt to its exposed surface. At the sights
marked by crosses in his sketch (Fig. 1), stimulation led to slowing
or cessation of spinal flexor action, a result which provided the
first demonstration of central neural inhibition. On returning to

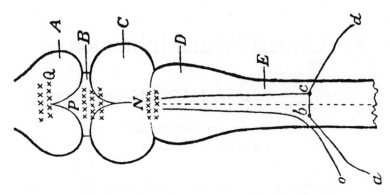

Fɪɢ. 1. Diagram of the central nervous system of the frog, from Sechenov (1935). Stimulation of the sites marked by crosses inhibited spinal reflexes, illustrating the hierarchy of neural levels and the dominance of higher over those below.

Moscow, Sechenov (1863) elaborated his findings in a monograph called *Reflexes of the Brain,* the centennary of the publication of which we celebrate this year.

In Sechenov's experiments, inhibition was exerted at the motor phase of the reflex act and, in the century since his discovery, Sherrington (1906) and others demonstrated the active nature and major integrative role of such inhibition in reflex motor performance; in particular, in reciprocal innervation, when excitation of the motor supply to one muscle group is characteristically associated with concomitant inhibition of its antagonist.

Moreover, in this past century, research techniques have advanced from salt on the brain to microelectrode recording from the interior of individual neurons. With this procedure, Eccles (1957) has recently determined that the mechanism of central neural inhibition is literally the reciprocal of excitation; that is, as the latter is the consequence of depolarization of the neuronal membrane to the point of generation of a self-propagating nerve impulse, so inhibition results from the contrasting hyperpolarization of the neuronal membrane, which becomes stabilized above a level permitting impulse generation. These epochal observations, made during antidromic inhibition of the

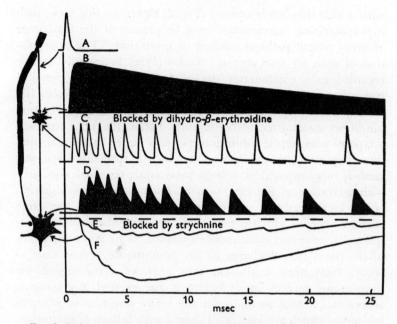

Fıg. 2. Diagram summarizing postulated sequence of events from an impulse in a motor axon to the inhibition of a motoneuron. All events are plotted on the same time scale and are referred to histological structures at the left. From Eccles (1957). Shown from above downward are: *A*, action potential in motor axon collateral; *B*, concentration of acetylcholine liberated at its pre-synaptic terminals; *C*, depolarization and repetitive firing of inhibitory interneurons induced by excitatory transmitter; *D*, concentration of inhibitory transmitter liberated at its presynaptic terminals; *E*, hyperpolarization of motoneuronal membrane induced by inhibitory transmitter; and *F*, its intensification by bombardment from many inhibitory interneurons.

cat's spinal motor neurons, additionally revealed the invariable involvement in the inhibitory process of an interneuron, itself excited by a collateral from the stimulated axon (Fig. 2, *left*). Eccles went on to propose the role of chemical commutators for such inhibitory interneurons which, themselves excited in the usual manner, elaborated at their own presynaptic terminals a distinctive inhibitory transmitter substance, which hyperpolarized the postsynaptic membrane of the next, or inhibited neuron, with which they made contact (Fig. 2, *right*). In this view, such hyperpolarizing interneurons must be present at the final stage of every neural pathway leading to inhibition. "The interpolation of such an interneuron," Eccles (1956) proposed, "can be regarded as a commutator device, for changing the chemical transmitter operating on the next cell in the pathway; cells liberating excitatory transmitter giving place to cells liberating inhibitory transmitter." More recently, Eccles (1961) has proposed a type of presynaptic inhibition, perhaps better called a depression of presynaptic excitation, in which a specialized synaptic knob is superimposed on a large presynaptic terminal associated with activation of the next neuron. Excitation of this superimposed knob leads to maintained depolarization of the large afferent fiber on which it ends, with resulting diminution of its spike potential and consequent depression of its synaptic efficacy to the point that discharge of the postsynaptic neuron fails to occur. Presynaptic inhibition thus provides a mechanism for suppressing afferent input before it has exerted any synaptic action and it thus accounts for the many instances of effective inhibition which are associated simply with failure of excitation, without hyperpolarization of the membrane of the postsynaptic cell.

EXTERNAL INHIBITION

A generation after Sechenov, a young medical graduate at St. Petersburg, named Pavlov, was strongly influenced by reading *The Reflexes of the Brain* and, in later study of conditional reflexes, he identified external and internal types of central inhibition. External inhibition was typified by cessation of behavior when novel extraneous stimulation evoked an orienting reflex. In Pavlov's (1927, 1928) original description of the orienting reflex, he wrote, "The appearance of any new stimulus immediately evokes the investigatory reflex, and the animal fixes all of its appropriate receptor organs upon the source of disturbance, pricking up its ears, fastening its gaze upon the disturbing agency, and sniffing the air. . . . In our laboratory, the neglect to provide against such external stimuli often led to a curious combination when I visited one of my coworkers. Having by himself established a new conditioned reflex, working in the room with a dog, the experimenter would invite me for a demonstration and then everything would go wrong and he would be unable to show anything at all. It was I who presented this extra stimulus; the investigatory reflex was immediately brought into play; the dog gazed at me and smelled me; and of course this was sufficient to inhibit every recently established reflex."

Work of the past two decades has determined the important role in central neural inhibition of nonspecific mechanisms distributed in the central core of the brain and, in the past few years, these central inhibitory systems have been shown to be capable of blocking sensory, as well as motor activity in the central nervous system. Hernandez-Péon (1961) has pointed out, as seen in Fig. 3, that "the reticular mechanisms of sensory filtering are formed by feedback loops, with an ascending segment from second order sensory neurons to the reticular formation, and a descending limb in the opposite direction. Such an arrange-

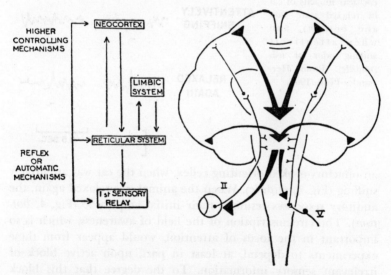

Fig. 3. Diagrammatic representation of mechanisms regulating sensory inflow to the brain. For simplicity, only the afferent visual and trigeminal pathways are shown. Corticifugal feedbacks to sensory relays and reticular formation are seen in heavy black. From Hernandez-Péon (1961).

ment prevents overactivation of sensory neurons and, therefore, an excessive bombardment of the brain by afferent impulses. Their exclusion takes place at the entrance gates of the central nervous system. The first sensory synapse functions as a valve where sensory filtering occurs."

In his work, Hernandez-Péon (1961) used implanted electrodes to record the response of the cat's cochlear nucleus to regularly recurring clicks. Prominent auditory potentials, in the relaxed or inattentive state (Fig. 4, *top*), were attenuated markedly during

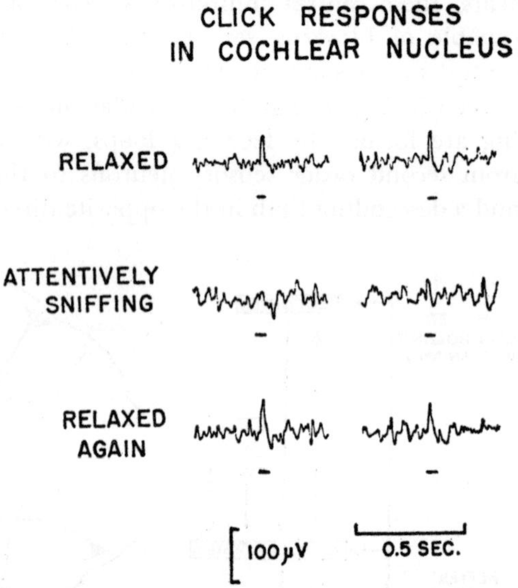

CLICK RESPONSES
IN COCHLEAR NUCLEUS

FIG. 4. Click responses recorded from implanted electrode in cochlear nucleus of cat in relaxed state (*top* and *bottom*), and when attentively sniffing odor of fish (*middle*). From Hernandez-Péon (1961).

an olfactory-evoked orienting reflex, when the cat was attentively sniffing (Fig. 4, *middle*). When the animal was relaxed again, the auditory responses resumed their initial amplitude (Fig. 4, *bottom*). The circumscription of the field of awareness, which is so important in the focus of attention, would appear from these experiments to depend, at least in part, upon active block of irrelevant sensory information. To the degree that this block is directly associated with a concomitant and opposing excitation, external or surround inhibition during the Pavlovian orienting reflex would similarly appear to follow closely the principle of reciprocal innervation identified earlier in motor integration.

HABITUATION

In another category of feedback control of input to the central nervous system, nonspecific core systems of the brain reduce or prevent central involvement by stereotyped, monotonously repeated stimuli. In the classic study by Sharpless and Jasper (1956), a typical pattern of habituation of the cat's EEG-arousal reaction begins with a prolonged evocation of arousal changes upon the initial presentation of a brief 500-cycle tone (Fig. 5, *top*). With recurring presentation of the same stimulus (Fig. 5, *successive records*), the duration of evoked activation became progressively reduced until, on the thirty-sixth trial, it was limited to the period of the stimulus. On the thirty-seventh trial, the arousal reaction no longer occurred at all and was said to be habituated.

This habituation was not the result of fatigue or other generalized impairment of the arousal mechanism for, in succeeding trials, tones of different pitch again evoked a full-blown response. Although the process obviously displayed specificity, in the sense that it involved neural mechanisms capable of pitch discrimination, such habituation could still be established after bilateral ablation of cortical auditory areas. In contrast to external inhibition, in which factors relating to EEG-arousal exclude irrelevant information, during habituation the monotonous presentation of irrelevant information led to disappearance of the EEG-arousal response itself. This consequence could not be attributed to block of input at lower sensory relays for, during habituation, auditory responses continued to be evoked in the cortex without reduction of amplitude (Sharpless & Jasper, 1956).

It has been proposed by Sokolov (1960) that the respective provocation of an orienting reflex or habituation is determined by the comparison of novel stimuli with neuronal models established in the cortex by previous stimulation. In Sokolov's view, the discordance between novel stimuli and an established model is responsible for triggering an orienting reflex. By contrast, the accordance with which stereotyped stimuli match the established model not only fails to evoke an orienting reflex but, by promoting inhibitory action, is additionally responsible for habituation. Sokolov's neuronal model (Fig. 6) is conceived as a cortical

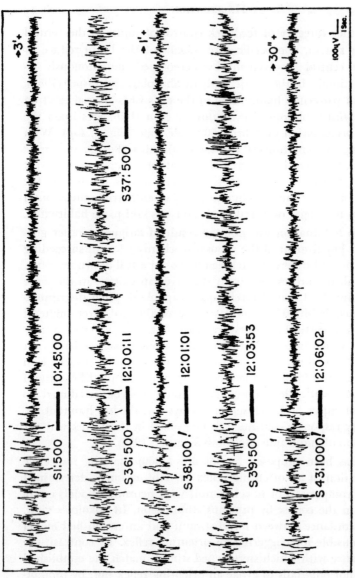

Fig. 5. Records of electrical activity from suprasylvian gyrus of cat, showing habituation of arousal reaction to 500-cycle tone (heavy bar below record), the number of presentations of which are designated by S 1, S 36, etc. (at the times indicated). Note habituation to 500-cycle tone on thirty-seventh and thirty-ninth trials, with marked arousal to novel, 100- and 1,000-cycle tones in same period. From Sharpless and Jasper (1956).

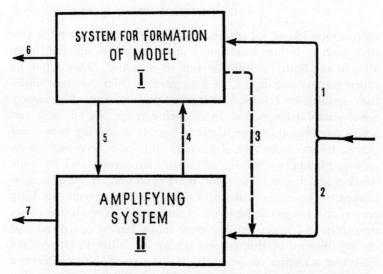

FIG. 6. Schema of the brain mechanisms involved in the orienting reflex. *I*. Cortical neuronal model; *II*. amplifying system in brain stem reticular formation. Functional connections are: *1*. specific pathway from receptor to cortical neuronal model; *2*. collateral afferent path to reticular formation; *3*. negative feedback from cortical model to afferent reticular collateral; *4*. ascending reticular activating pathway to cortex; *5*. cortico-reticular connections signalling concordance or discordance between afferent stimuli and the cortical neuronal model; *6*. corticifugal pathways for specific responses; *7*. reticulofugal pathways for nonspecific somatic and visceral responses. From Sokolov (1960).

cell assembly that preserves information about the modality, intensity, duration, and other parameters of earlier stimuli, with which analogous aspects of novel stimulation may be compared. According to his hypothesis, the orienting reflex is evoked whenever, upon such comparison, features of the novel stimulus do not coincide with those of the established model. This discordance, it is proposed, evokes the orienting reflex. In the contrasting situation, when novel stimuli are accordant with the established neuronal model, the orienting reflex is not induced. Moreover, upon repetition, such accordance of stimulus and model is proposed to inhibit central arousal systems of the brain and so promote habituation.

INTERNAL INHIBITION

In continuation of his studies, Pavlov (1927, 1928) found it possible both to induce conditional motor responses and, additionally, to establish "a learning not to respond." This latter he called internal inhibition, to distinguish it from external inhibition, typified by cessation of learned performance when strong, novel stimulation evoked an orienting reflex. In an alert and active dog responding regularly to signals, a striking behavioral change follows induction of internal inhibition. Secretomotor responses gradually diminish and cease. Drowsiness and lassitude develop and become more and more profound. If the process is pushed to the extreme, the eyes close, the head droops, the body relaxes and hangs on the loops of the stand, as the animal passes into sleep and emits an occasional snore. Pavlov conceived that the significance of this process lay in its ability to perfect the analyzing activities of the brain, making possible more effective adaptation to the environment. Additionally, he proposed that internal inhibition provided opportunity for refreshment and recovery, after excitation and fatigue. Upon irradiating and becoming generalized in the brain, he held, it was responsible for sleep.

THALAMO-CORTICAL MECHANISMS FOR INTERNAL INHIBITION

Following Pavlov's contributions, two succeeding discoveries have been of greatest significance for the proposal that a diffusely projecting, thalamo-cortical EEG-synchronizing system constitutes the neural mechanism for internal inhibition. The first of these, by Hess (1944), reported the induction of behavioral sleep by low-frequency, electrical stimulation of the paramedial thalamic region of the cat (Fig. 7). Later EEG studies showed this induced sleep to be associated with large-amplitude, slow waves, and spindle bursts characteristic of light sleep, both in animals and in man.

In a second major contribution, Morison and Dempsey (1942) found that low-frequency stimulation of this midline thalamic region evoked a progressively recruiting, wavelike response in the cortical EEG (Fig. 8, *A*). These widely distributed recruiting re-

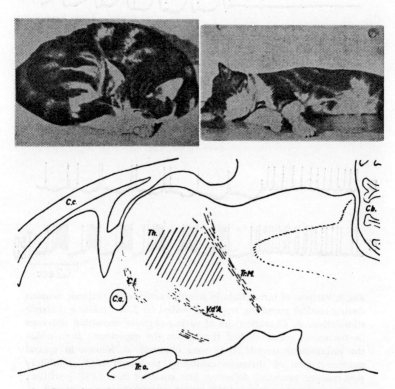

Fig. 7. Sleep induced by low-frequency thalamic stimulation (*above*), with the effective zone marked (*below*) by shading on a parasagittal section of the cat's brain stem. From Hess (1944).

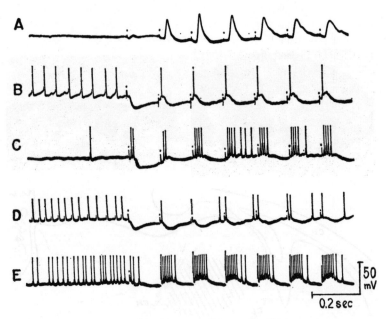

FIG. 8. Patterns of intracellularly recorded activities of thalamic neurons during cortical recruiting responses evoked by 7/sec. midline thalamic stimulation. *A*. Characteristics of surface-negative recruiting responses in the motor cortex elicited throughout the experiment from which the intracellular records (B–E) were obtained. *B*. Neuron in ventral anterior region of thalamus exhibiting prolonged IPSP (inhibitory post-synaptic potential) following first stimulus then EPSP (excititory post-synaptic potential) – IPSP sequences with successive stimuli. *C*. Relatively quiescent ventrolateral neuron develops double discharge with first stimulus. The ensuing IPSP is succeeded by another evoked EPSP and cell discharge. *D*. Neuron with discharge characteristics similar to that shown in *B*. *E*. Neuron in intralaminar region exhibiting an initial prolonged IPSP that interrupts spontaneous discharges. The second and all successive stimuli evoke prolonged EPSP's with repetitive discharges that are terminated by IPSP's. From Purpura and Shofer (1963).

sponses resembled spontaneous spindle bursts; and the two inter-
acted with one another, indicating the involvement of a common
mechanism. From their studies, Morison and Dempsey proposed
the existence of a nonspecific thalamo-cortical system, arising
from midline and intralaminar nuclei, distinct from specific affer-
ent projections of the relay thalamic nuclei (Fig. 9, *left*). More

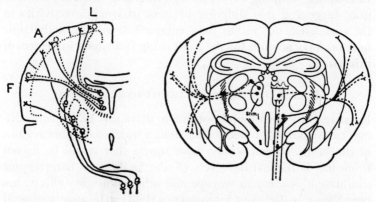

Fig. 9. *Left:* Diagram showing independence of specific and nonspecific
thalamo-cortical projections. From Morison and Dempsey (1942). *Right:*
Diagram showing independence of nonspecific thalamo-cortical system
for EEG synchronization and recruiting responses (*left*) and that relay-
ing ascending reticular influences for EEG arousal (*right*). From Tissot
and Monnier (1959).

recently, Monnier and his associates (1960) have proposed the
existence of dual and reciprocally antagonistic components with-
in the nonspecific thalamo-cortical projection itself (Fig. 9, *right*).
One of these, capable of firing at rapid-stimulus frequencies, was
suggested to form a relay for ascending reticular influences
leading to EEG arousal; while the second, which fired best at low-
stimulus frequencies, was proposed to be responsible for recruit-
ing responses, spindle bursts, and synchronization of the EEG.

Most recently, Purpura and his associates (1962, 1963) have
obtained intracellular records from thalamic neurons during low-
frequency stimulation of the midline thalamic system. Synchro-
nization of thalamo-cortical electrical activity (Fig. 8, *A—E*) was
usually associated with patterns of long-lasting post-synaptic po-

tentials, consisting of short-latency depolarization and firing, responsible for the cortical recruiting response, followed by long-latency hyperpolarization or inhibition, which effectively blocked excitation and rendered the elements unresponsive to stimulation from other sources. In Purpura's experiments, the same elements participating in recruiting responses were also involved in the EEG-desynchronizing effects of high-frequency thalamic stimulation, suggesting that differing patterns of synaptic activities in the same elements, rather than antagonistic groups of thalamic neurons, may account for the contrasting functional influences of this system.

BULBAR DRIVING OF THALAMO-CORTICAL SYSTEM

It has recently been found possible to drive this EEG-synchronizing, thalamo-cortical mechanism from a number of other regions of the brain. Recent studies have shown that it can be driven from the bulbo-pontile levels of the brainstem. Baroreceptor stimulation, leading to syncope and other inhibitory effects, has been shown by Dell and his associates (1961) to be associated with generalized synchronization of the EEG. In agreement, Moruzzi (1960) has evoked large slow waves and spindle bursts in the EEG by low-frequency stimulation of the solitary tract and bulbo-reticular formation. When this bulbar synchronizing mechanism is eliminated by transection through the pons or by reversible pharmacological block, an initially synchronized EEG gives way to a pattern of EEG arousal (Fig. 10). This bulbo-pontile, EEG synchronizing and internally inhibiting influence, capable of interoceptor excitation, would seem from its lowly position to be phylogenetically old. Possibly it is directed toward influencing visceral function generally through the body by reducing the excitability of the brain.

SATIETY AND INTERNAL INHIBITION

Other mechanisms capable of driving the synchronizing thalamo-cortical system are present in the hypothalamus, where they appear to be related to the regulation of innate behavior and to related control of pituitary function. In the study of feeding

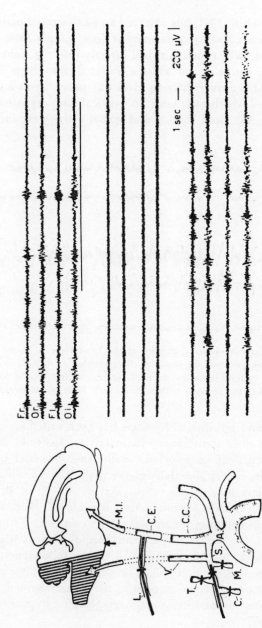

Fig. 10. Continuous records (*right*) show EEG arousal following inactivation of lower brain stem by selective injection (signal) of barbiturate into the vertebral circulation (*left*). From Magni, Moruzzi, Rossi, and Zanchetti (1959).

behavior, Anokhin (1961) has observed an EEG arousal pattern in the frontal cortex and hypothalamus of dogs, hungry from deprivation of food. When food is tubed directly into the stomach of these hungry animals, and glucose injected into their bloodstream, this EEG arousal pattern gives way promptly to a record of pronounced synchrony both in cortical and hypothalamic channels (Fig. 11). Both feeding and sexual activity are initiated

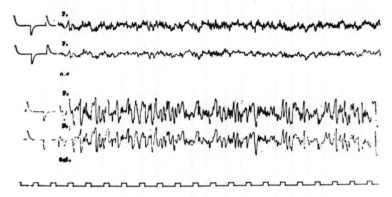

FIG. 11. Records of electrical activity of the frontal cortex of the cat under urethane anaesthesia, showing the transition from EEG desynchronization in hunger (*above*) to EEG synchrony after glucose injection and filling the stomach with milk (*below*). From Anokhin (1961).

by appetites and terminated by what has been called satiety. In showing how their termination—in inactivity, lassitude, drowsiness, and often sleep—is associated with synchrony and spindle bursting in the electrical activity of the brain, these findings suggest that satiety may be the expression of a type of internal inhibition which, after consummation is achieved, plays an important role in bringing innate behavior to an end. Within the hypothalamus, the region of the ventromedial nucleus is importantly implicated in the induction of satiety following feeding (Hetherington & Ranson, 1940). The direct stimulation of this region stops feeding behavior, even in the hungry animal; while lesions here are followed by hyperphagia, leading to pronounced obesity (Fig. 12).

Fig. 12. Photos showing obesity in the rat following lesions in the hypothalamic ventromedial nucleus (*top*), by comparison with the litter mate control (*bottom*). From Hetherington and Ranson (1940).

In a study of the neuroendocrine control of sexual behavior, Sawyer and Kawakami (1961) have observed a period of several minutes following coitus, in which the female rabbit displays a languid relaxation and inactivity, resembling internal inhibition, which terminates abruptly in a rebound burst of feeding (Fig. 13). During this period, the animal's EEG first displays cortical spindle bursts, followed by the pattern of paradoxical sleep. In an appropriately primed rabbit, the administration of gonadotrophic hormones leads to a similar inhibition of behavior, which is likewise accompanied by the EEG changes just described. Such endocrine potentiation of this mechanism suggests that an elevated titer of hormones in the circulation of the brain may, by promoting internal inhibition, reduce the activity of hypothalamic neural systems initiating the secretion of pituitary trophic hormones. If so, this mechanism may provide a basis for the negative feedback control of pituitary function, in which there is

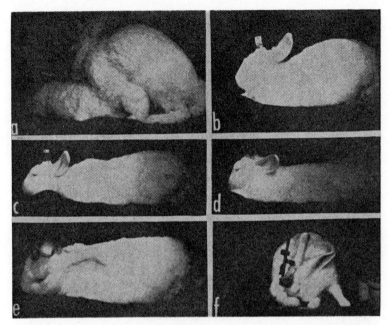

FIG. 13. Serial photos showing reduction of behavior of the female rabbit following coitus (*a*). In (*b*), the eyes close and at this time frontal spindle bursts appear. In *c–e*, the head sinks to the floor, the ears droop and behavioral depression is complete; at this time, hippocampal hypersynchrony is pronounced and the animal is deeply asleep. In *f*, the animal suddenly recovers and feeds ravenously for a few moments. From Sawyer and Kawakami (1961).

increasingly compelling evidence for the presence of a central neural stage.

In its role in innate behavior, as well as in regulation of endocrine and visceral function, the hypothalamus is intimately related to limbic structures of the forebrain, and is functionally connected with them through the septal and preoptic regions. Recently, Sterman and Clemente (1962) have found that bilateral, low-frequency stimulation of the preoptic region is an exceedingly potent and expeditious way of inducing widespread EEG spindling and behavioral sleep (Fig. 14), and these alterations appear to be mediated by the diffuse thalamocortical system.

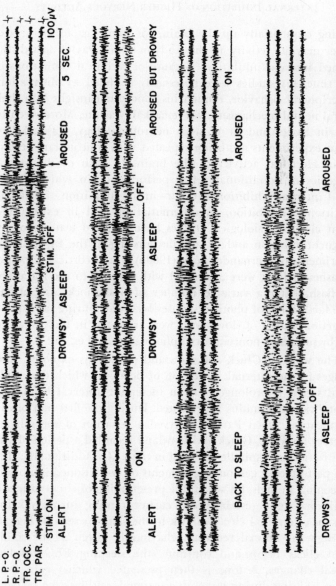

Fig. 14. Continuous records showing EEG and behavioral sleep induced repeatedly by low-frequency, bilateral stimulation of the preoptic region of the cat. From Sterman and Clemente (1961).

INTERNAL INHIBITION OF HIGHER NERVOUS ACTIVITY

Moving sequentially up the brain, we come last to features of higher nervous activity, in the study of which Pavlov first distinguished internal inhibition. Because of technical limitations of that time, his studies were necessarily confined to observations of peripheral behavior, though his conceptual insight into their central neural mechanisms was remarkably astute. More recently, both in Soviet and in Western neurophysiology, classical Pavlovian experiments are being repeated with concomitant recording of electrical activity of the brain. In each of the several categories of conditional reflex performance in which Pavlov found internal inhibition to occur—in the inhibition of delay, in conditioned inhibition, in differentiation, and in extinction—recent electrophysiological studies have revealed features of hypersynchronization and/or spindle bursting in the EEG. In the experiments of Hernandez-Péon (1960b), visual cortical responses to flashes of light were associated with a shock to the leg at the last flash. After a variable number of flash-shock associations, some facilitation of photic responses occurred. During subsequent extinction, bursts of slow waves were triggered in increasing degree by successive nonreinforced photic stimuli (Fig. 15).

The work of Gluck and Rowland (1959) has explored EEG changes in the internal inhibition of delay, in which the conditional signal is prolonged for an increasing interval before the unconditioned stimulus is presented. During the first half of this prolongation, when Pavlov observed a cessation of the salivary secretory response, Gluck and Rowland recorded a period of synchronization and spindle bursting in the EEG. Additionally, they have performed ingenious experiments on conditioned inhibition in sleeping animals, for whom the presentation of clicks formed a conditional signal (established in earlier training during wakefulness) for a terminal electric shock to the skin. As seen in Fig. 16, although the animal remains behaviorally asleep as the conditional clicks begin and continue, the sleeping EEG displays arousal changes. A tone is then presented which (again from earlier training during wakefulness) signals withholding of painful reinforcement. Shortly after this tone begins, the EEG record

FIG. 15. Electrical activity of the visual cortex of a cat, previously conditioned to four flashes of light at 1/sec., associated with a shock to the leg. The numbers indicate the trials without reinforcement. During extinction, note that photic stimulation increasingly triggers spindle bursts. From Hernandez-Péon (1960).

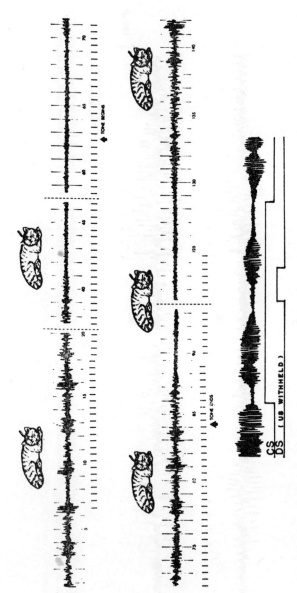

Fig. 16. Continuous record of cortical electrical activity in a sleeping cat, with changes diagrammed below. In the record, note that EEG arousal induced by presentation of the conditional stimulus (clicks, marked by vertical lines below record) is twice interrupted by spindle bursts. The first group of bursts is associated with inhibition of delay, and the second with presentation of a differential stimulus (tone, the onset and conclusion of which is indicated by arrows), signalling withholding of painful reinforcement. When the conditional signal ends, the EEG returns to a sleeping pattern. From Gluck and Rowland (1959).

returns once more to the sleeping type, to arouse again upon conclusion of the tone. Last, as the warning clicks finally end, without a shock, the EEG returns to sleep and gets terminally into line with behavior.

In summation, these many contributions point to the existence of a nonspecific, thalamo-cortical system, the low-frequency excitation of which evokes large slow waves as well as recruiting responses and spindle bursts in the EEG. These characteristically bear a close relation to internal inhibition, behavioral drowsiness, and sleep, although they can display dissociation from such behavior. Differentiable components exist in this thalamo-cortical system and are capable of being driven more or less independently by inputs from a number of other parts of the brain. Involvement of this mechanism from bulbo-pontile sources may be designed to effect a general reduction of visceral processes. Its excitation from hypothalamic and limbic structures appears to provide a means of terminating innate behavior by satiety as well as to serve in feedback control of pituitary function. When activated from the basal ganglia and cerebral cortex, this system appears to manage all the Pavlovian categories of internal inhibition of higher nervous activity, including that of sleep itself.

If the inferences drawn from these many conclusions are correct, it is now possible to identify a thalamo-cortical mechanism for internal inhibition, capable of modifying activity of the brain partially or globally, so that its sensory, motor, and higher nervous functions become reduced and cease. The consequences of the action of this mechanism are the opposite of those of the ascending reticular activating system for internal excitation (Magoun, 1963). The principle of reciprocal innervation proposed by Sherrington (1906) to account for spinal-reflex integration would additionally appear relevant to the manner in which these two higher antagonistic neural mechanisms determine the alternating patterns of brain activity manifest as wakefulness and light sleep.

SLEEP

In broad view, our daily existence can be divided into recurring periods of fundamentally opposite behavior, one of which, wakefulness, bears a cosmic relation to the lighted portion of the earth's ceaseless rotation with respect to the glowing sun. We spend the more productive and interesting two-thirds of our lives in a state of wakefulness. By contrast, sleep is related to the darkened portion of the earth's daily spin, in which we spend the more unproductive third of our lives. It has been proposed that sleep may be necessary for recovery from the excitation and fatigue of wakefulness, a concept elegantly expressed by Shakespeare, when he made reference to "Sleep, which knitteth up the ravelled sleeve of care."

The sleeping state is characterized by a general predominance of inactivity, within which there can be noted the breakdown of all effective relations of the individual with the external world: on the afferent side by the absence of perception and, on the efferent, by loss of capacity for most motor performance, except that maintaining vital processes. Subjective experience is not totally lacking, however, for about twenty per cent of sleep is spent in dreaming, in which sequences of sensory, motor, and associational activity, often strongly flavored with emotion, occur along with rapid movements of the eyeballs and twitches of the extremities. Consolidation of such dream experiences into memory and their subesquent recall is much reduced by comparison with subjective experience in wakefulness.

DIFFERENTIATION OF LIGHT AND DEEP SLEEP

Current study points to the existence of two differentiable stages of sleep, served by distinct neural mechanisms which appear respectively to reduce the activity of cortical and subcortical levels of the brain. The first of these is light sleep, developing from Pavlovian internal inhibition and served by the nonspecific thalamo-cortical system responsible for large amplitude slow-waves and spindle bursts characteristic of the synchronized EEG.

A second stage of sleep, recently identified by Dement and Kleitman (1957), Dement (1958), Jouvet (1962), Rossi (1961), Hubel (1960), and others, is called deep, activated, or paradoxical sleep. It is characterized by low-voltage, fast discharge in the electrocorticogram and by a theta rhythm in the hippocampus, which are exceedingly similar to the EEG patterns of alert wakefulness.

This stage of deep sleep is never reached directly from wakefulness but only occurs after passing first through the light slow-wave thalamo-cortical stage (Fig. 17). The most marked

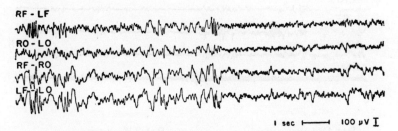

RF - LF

RO - LO

RF - RO

LF - LO

⊢ 1 sec ⊣ ⊢ 100 µV I

FIG. 17. Records of cortical electrical activity of a sleeping cat, showing rapid spontaneous transition from high-voltage slow (*left*) to low-voltage fast (*right*) sleep. Light sleep had begun ten minutes before; deep sleep, with twitching, continued for five minutes after the transition shown, when the animal was awakened by an auditory stimulus. From Hubel (1960).

somato-vegetative changes in sleep—the complete relaxation of postural tone in the skeletal musculature, together with miosis, slowing of the heart and fall in blood pressure—have all been associated with this stage of deep sleep. Contrary to the earlier conclusions of Dement and Kleitman (1957), this deep, paradoxical, activated stage of sleep has recently been proposed by Jouvet (1962) to be that in which dreaming occurs.

The adjective "deep" applied to this stage of sleep, implies that a greater intensity of stimulation is required to induce wakefulness, whether tested by peripheral afferent stimulation or, as seen in Fig. 18, from Hara et al. (1960), by direct, recticular stimulation, when a much higher voltage is needed to arouse an animal from the deep stage of sleep than from the light stage. Additionally, Rossi et al. (1961) has shown that electrocortical recruiting responses, evoked by stimulation of the nonspecific thalamic nuclei during light sleep (Fig. 19), can no longer be elicited during deep sleep. In such a situation, the induction of central barbiturate anesthesia, blocking lower brain stem function, frees the thalamo-cortical system, so that recruiting responses can once more be induced.

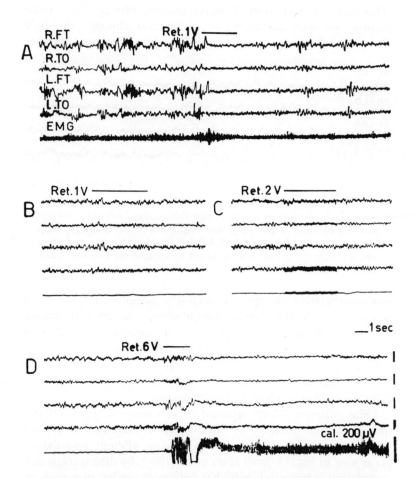

Fig. 18. Records of cortical electrical activity and EMG of a cat with stimulating electrodes implanted in the midbrain reticular formation. During light sleep (*A*), arousal is evoked by 1 V, reticular stimulation. In *B* and *C*, 1 and 2 V, reticular stimulation is unable to arouse the animal from deep sleep. In *D*, 6 V, reticular stimulation awakens the animal from deep sleep, as seen best in return of tonic background in EMG. From Hara, Favale, Rossi, and Sacco (1960).

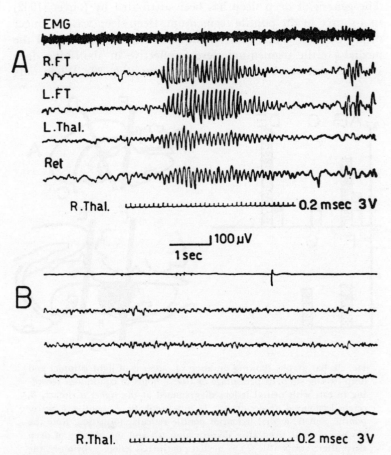

FIG. 19. Records of EMG and electrical activity of cortex, thalamus and midbrain reticular formation, showing large amplitude recruiting responses, induced by low-frequency stimulation of intralaminar thalamic nuclei during light sleep (*A*), and absence of responses to similar stimulation during deep sleep (*B*). From Rossi et al. (1961).

PONTILE MECHANISM FOR DEEP SLEEP

The genesis of deep sleep has been attributed by Jouvet (1962) to a source in the pontile tegmentum. Deep sleep was no longer displayed after transections of the pons and focal lesions of the medial pontile tegmentum were as effective in abolishing deep sleep as were more extensive transections (Fig. 20). When only

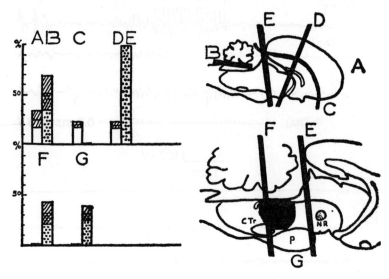

FIG. 20. Bar graphs showing duration of patterns of light (stipple) and deep (white) sleep, as percentage of twelve hours of continuous recording in cats with neural lesions diagrammed at the *right: A.* intact, *B.* cerebellectomized, *C.* decorticate, *D.* mesencephalic, *E.* pontile, *F.* retropontile, and *G.* medial lesions of pontile reticular formation. Note the absence of light sleep after decortication (*C*) and the absence of deep sleep after retropontile (*F*) or medial pontile (*G*) lesions. Obviously, the cortical EEG is not influenced during deep sleep in mesencephalic and pontile cats. Deep sleep is distinguished, in these preparations, by changes in pontile electrical activity and in the EMG. From Jouvet (1961).

the ponto-bulbar brain stem remained connected with the cord, the peripheral manifestations of deep sleep—the total loss of postural tone, slowing of the heart, and fall of blood pressure—continued to be manifest periodically. Jouvet proposes that ascending influences of this pontile system run forward through the ventral and medial part of the upper brain stem, independent of reticulo-cortical influences for generalized wakefulness.

GENERAL FEATURES OF LIGHT AND DEEP SLEEP

The several terms that have been used to differentiate these two stages of sleep make reference to their different distinguishing features. The terms *thalamic* and *pontile* (or rhombencephalic) sleep refer to the sites of the inhibitory mechanisms proposed to be involved. The terms *light* and *deep* sleep refer to the increased difficulty in awakening the sleeping animal by peripheral afferent or direct reticular stimulation during deep, as compared with light sleep. The terms *slow-wave* and *fast-wave* (or activated) sleep refer to the patterns of electrocortical activity which characterize the two stages. The term *paradoxical* sleep refers to the surprising resemblance between the EEG pattern of deep sleep and that of wakefulness. It seems possible to make a synthesis of these several designations, and additionally to relate them to the presence or absence of subjective dreaming, if emphasis is placed upon the parts of the brain which undergo inhibition during each stage of sleep, rather than upon the site of the inhibiting mechanisms or other features.

It can be proposed that in the light, slow-wave stage of sleep, cortical function is predominantly impaired. In this stage, synchronization of the cortical EEG may be the consequence of prolonged hyperpolarizing post-synaptic potentials, blocking the spontaneous activity of the nonspecific thalamo-cortical projection system and rendering it unresponsive to excitatory drives (Purpura et al., 1962, 1963). These changes may, in turn, contribute to gating other neuronal discharge into ineffective firing patterns (Calma & Arduini, 1954). Arousal from this stage of sleep is relatively easy, for other subcortical mechanisms are predominantly uninvolved. Subjective dreaming is lacking, for during pronounced EEG synchronization, cortical function appears inadequate to support subjective experience.

Contrastingly, it can be proposed that in the deep, fast-wave stage of sleep, subcortical function is predominantly impaired.

The absence of slow waves in the electrocortical record is attributable to inhibition of the nonspecific thalamo-cortical synchronizing system, which is no longer excitable, even to direct stimulation. Arousal from this stage is difficult because of inhibition of the ascending reticular activating system. As noted, much higher than usual intensities of afferent or direct reticular stimulation are necessary to induce general wakefulness in this deep stage of sleep. The paradoxical pattern of EEG arousal characteristic of this deep stage of sleep appears adequate, however, to support degrees of subjective experience, including intense emotion, in dreaming. The pronounced hypersynchrony of electrical activity observed in limbic structures during deep sleep suggests that differences in hippocampal activity may be of great significance here, and perhaps especially so in relation to memory processing and the exceedingly brief period of recall usually associated with dreaming. The lack of motor manifestations, except for eye movements and occasional twitching of face or limbs, during dreaming, may be attributed either to inhibition of the reticulo-spinal facilitatory system or, conversely, to excitation of the bulbar reticulo-spinal system capable of widespread inhibition of lower motor activity.

More generally, it has long been known that varying degrees of wakefulness exist and, from these exciting recent advances, it is no longer possible to consider sleep a unitary category of behavior. From current work, two stages of sleep can be differentiated: by distinctive patterns of electro-cortical activity, by differing levels of arousability, and by the presence or absence of dreaming. The degree of involvement of somato-vegetative alterations is also distinctive. These categories of light, slow-wave and of deep, activated sleep, can seemingly be attributed respectively to the inhibition of predominantly cortical, and of predominantly subcortical levels of the brain.

REFERENCES

Anokhin, P. K. The multiple ascending influences of the subcortical centers on the cerebral cortex. In M. A. B. Brazier (Ed.), *Brain and behavior.* Washington: AIBS, 1961.

Calma, I., & Arduini, A. Spontaneous and induced activity in pyramidal units. *J. Neurophysiol.,* 1954, **17,** 321–335.

Dell, P., Bonvallet, M., & Hugelin, A. Mechanisms of reticular deactivation. In G. E. W. Wolstenholme & M. O'Connor (Eds.), *The nature of sleep.* London: Churchill, Ltd., 1961. Pp. 86–107.

Dement, W. The effect of dream deprivation. *Science,* 1960, **131,** 1705–1707.

Dement, W., & Kleitman, N. Cyclic variations of EEG during sleep and their relation to eye movements, body motility and dreaming. *EEG Clin. Neurophysiol.,* 1957, **9,** 673–690.

Diamond, S., Balvin, R. S., & Diamond, F. R. *Inhibition and choice.* New York: Harper & Row, 1963.

Eccles, J. C. *The physiology of nerve cells.* Baltimore: The Johns Hopkins Press, 1957.

Eccles, J. C. The mechanism of synaptic transmission. *Ergbn. Physiol.,* 1961, **51,** 299–430.

Gluck, H., & Rowland, V. Defensive conditioning of electrographic arousal with delayed and differentiated auditory stimuli. *EEG Clin. Neurophysiol.,* 1959, **11,** 485–496.

Hara, T., Favale, E., Rossi, G. F., & Sacco, G. Richerche sull'attivita elettrica cerebrale durante il sonno nel gatto. *Riv. Neurol.,* 1960, **30,** 448–460.

Hernandez-Péon, R. Neurophysiological correlates of habituation and other manifestations of plastic inhibition. In H. H. Jasper & G. O. Smirnov (Eds.), *Moscow colloquium on EEG and higher nervous activity. EEG Clin. Neurophysiol. Suppl.,* 1960, **13,** 101–114.

Hernandez-Péon, R. Reticular mechanisms of sensory control. In W. Rosenblith (Ed.), *Sensory Communication.* New York: M. I. T. Wiley, 1961. Pp. 497–520.

Hess, W. R. Das Schlafsyndrom als Folge dienzephaler Reizung. *Helv. Physiol. Acta,* 1944, **2,** 305–344.

Hetherington, A. W., & Ranson, S. W. Hypothalamic lesions and adiposity in the rat. *Anat. Rec.,* 1940, **78,** 149–172.

Hubel, D. H. Electrocorticograms in cats during natural sleep. *Arch. Ital. Biol.,* 1960, **98,** 171–181.

Jouvet, M. Recherches sur les structures nerveuses et les mecanismes responsibles des differentes phases du sommeil physiologique. *Arch. Ital. Biol.,* 1962, 100, 125–206.

Magni, F., Moruzzi, G., Rossi, G. F., & Zanchetti, A. EEG arousal following inactivation of lower brain stem by selective injection of barbiturate into the vertebral circulation. *Arch. Ital. Biol.,* 1959, 97, 33–46.

Magoun, H. W. *The waking brain* (2nd ed.). Springfield, Ill.: C. C. Thomas, 1963.

Monnier, M., Kalbere, M., & Krupp, P. Functional antagonism between diffuse reticular and intralaminary recruiting projections in the medial thalamus. *Exper Neurol.,* 1960, 2, 271–289.

Morison, R. S., & Dempsey, E. W. A study of thalamo-cortical relations. *Amer. J. Physiol.,* 1942, 135, 281–292.

Moruzzi, G. Synchronizing influences of the brain stem and the inhibitory mechanisms underlying the production of sleep by sensory stimulation. In H. H. Jasper & G. D. Smirnov (Eds.), Moscow colloquium on EEG and higher nervous activity. *EEG Clin. Neurophysiol. Suppl.,* 1960, 13, 231–257.

Pavlov, I. P. *Conditioned reflexes.* An investigation of the physiological activity of the cerebral cortex. In G. V. Anrep (Trans. & Ed.). London: Oxford Univer. Press, 1927.

Pavlov, I. P. *Lectures on conditioned reflexes.* Vols. I & II. In W. H. Gantt (Trans. & Ed.). New York: Internat. Publ., 1928, 1941.

Purpura, D. P., & Cohen, B. Intracellular recording from thalamic neurons during recruiting responses. *J. Neurophysiol.,* 1962, 25, 621–635.

Purpura, D. P., & Shofer, R. J. Intracellular recording from thalamic neurons during reticulocortical activation. *J. Neurophysiol.,* 1963, in press.

Rossi, G. F., Favale, E., Hara, T., Giussani, A., & Sacco, G. Researches on the nervous mechanisms underlying deep sleep in the cat. *Arch. Ital. Biol.,* 1961, 99, 270–292.

Sawyer, C. H., & Kawakami, M. Interactions between the central nervous system and hormones influencing ovulation. In C. A. Vilee (Ed.), *Control of ovulation.* New York: Pergamon Press, 1961. Pp. 79–97.

Sechenov, I. M. *Physiologische Studien über die Hemmungsmechanismen für Reflexthätigkeit des Ruckenmarks im Gehirne des Frosches.* Berlin: Hirschwald, 1863.

Sechenov, I. M. Reflexes of the brain (1863). In A. A. Subkov (Trans. & Ed.), *Selected works.* Moscow: State Pub. House for Biol. & Med. Lit., 1935.

Sharpless, S., & Jasper, H. H. Habituation of the arousal reaction. *Brain*, 1956, 79, 655–680.

Sherrington, C. S. *The integrative action of the nervous system.* New Haven: Yale Univer. Press, 1906.

Sokolov, E. N. Neuronal models and the orienting reflex. In M. A. B. Brazier (Ed.), *CNS and Behavior III.* New York: Josiah Macy, Jr. Found., 1960. Pp. 187–276.

Sterman, M. B., & Clemente, C. D. Forebrain inhibiting mechanisms; cortical synchronization induced by basal forebrain stimulation. *Exper. Neurol.*, 1962, 6, 91–102.(a)

Sterman, M. B., & Clemente, C. D. Sleep patterns induced by basal forebrain stimulation in the behaving cat. *Exper. Neurol.*, 1962, 6, 103–117.(b)

Tissot, R., & Monnier, M. Dualité du system thalmique de projection diffuse. *EEG Clin. Neurophysiol.*, 1959, 11, 675–686.

Indexes

Subject Index

Author Index

DATE DUE